Scholastic
Read-Aloud Anthology

by Janet Allen and Patrick Daley

SCHOLASTIC
Teaching
Resources

New York ✳ Toronto ✳ London ✳ Auckland ✳ Sydney

Mexico City ✳ New Delhi ✳ Hong Kong ✳ Buenos Aires

Dedication

For all the teachers who make words come alive for their students by reading aloud to them each day. Thank you for creating and sustaining the literate lives of <u>all</u> our children.

Patrick and Janet would also like to thank the following teachers, editors, and students who suggested, read, and rated every selection in this book: Becky Bone, Madelyn Carson, Chris Cinelli, Anne Cobb, Patricia D'Agostino, Michael Dahlie, Virginia Dooley, Linnette Ellis, Kim Feltes, Christy Jehn, Jennifer Johnson, Tonya Leslie, Michael Leviton, Noelle Morris, Dr. Debi Sulzer, Angela Wade, Elizabeth Ward.

Acknowledgments

Every effort has been made to contact copyright holders for permission to reproduce borrowed material. We regret any oversights that may have occurred and will be pleased to rectify them in subsequent reprints of the work.

"All the Cats in the World" by Sonia Levitin. Copyright © 1982. Reprinted by permission of Toni Mendez Agency for the author.

"A Teacher's Lament" and "There's a Cobra in the Bathroom" by Kalli Dakos. Reprinted by permission of Simon & Schuster Books for Young Readers, an imprint of Simon & Schuster Children's Publishing Division from IF YOU'RE NOT HERE, PLEASE RAISE YOUR HAND by Kalli Dakos. Text copyright © 1990 by Kalli Dakos.

"A Mouthful" by Paul Jennings. Reprinted from UNCOVERED! WEIRD, WEIRD STORIES by Paul Jennings. Copyright © 1998 Greenleaves Pts. Ltd.

"The Escape" by J. B. Stamper. Copyright © 1999 by J.B. Stamper. Reprinted by permission of the author.

"Around the River Bend" by Sherry Garland from SCHOLASTIC SCOPE, December 13, 1996. Copyright © 1996 by Sherry Garland. Reprinted by permission of Sherry Garland and Scholastic Inc.

"New Kid" by Patricia Hermes. Copyright © 1999 by Patricia Hermes. Reprinted by permission of the author.

"My Rows and Piles of Coins" by Tololwa M. Mollel. Text copyright © 1999 by Tololwa M. Mollel. Reprinted by permission of Clarion Books, a division of Houghton Mifflin Company. All rights reserved.

"I Never Said I Wasn't Difficult" and "The Dog Ate My Homework" by Sara Holbrook. Copyright © 1996 by Sara Holbrook. Reprinted by arrangement with Wordsong, Boyds Mills Press, Inc.

"Testing New Waters" by Sara Holbrook. Copyright © 2002 by Sara Holbrook. Reprinted by arrangement with Windsong, Boyds Mills Press, Inc.

"I Have a Dream" by Martin Luther King, Jr.

"Just a Pigeon" by Dennis Brindell Fradin. Copyright © 1996 by Dennis Brindell Fradin. Reprinted by permission of the author.

"The Lottery" from THE LOTTERY AND OTHER STORIES by Shirley Jackson. Copyright © 1948, 1949 by Shirley Jackson. Copyright renewed © 1976, 1977 by Laurence Hyman, Barry Hyman, Mrs. Sarah Webster and Mrs. Joanne Schnurer. Reprinted by arrangement with Farrar, Straus and Giroux, Inc.

"Eleven" from WOMAN HOLLERING CREEK AND OTHER STORIES by Sandra Cisneros. Copyright © 1991 by Sandra Cisneros. Reprinted by arrangement with Random House, Inc.

"Sick" from WHERE THE SIDEWALK ENDS by Shel Silverstein. Copyright © 1974 by Evil Eye Music, Inc. Used by permission of HarperCollins Publishers.

"Only a Dollar's Work" by Herma Werner. Copyright © 1993 by Herma Werner.

"Autobiography in Five Short Chapters" from THERE'S A HOLE IN MY SIDEWALK by Portia Nelson. Copyright © 1993 by Portia Nelson. Reprinted by permission of Beyond Words Publishing, Inc., Hillsboro, OR.

"Roger's Swim" from AMAZING TRUE STORIES by Don L. Wulffson. Copyright © 1991 by Don L. Wulffson. Used by permission of Cobblehill Books, an affiliate of Dutton Children's Books, an imprint of Penguin Putnam Books for Young Readers, a division of Penguin Putnam Inc.

"Ballad of Birmingham" by Dudley Randall, from THE BLACK POETS. Copyright © 1971. Published by Bantam, Reprinted by permission of the author.

"Why My Homework Is Late" by Rebecca Kai Dotlich from NO MORE HOMEWORK! NO MORE TESTS! Selected by Bruce Lansky. Copyright © 1996 by Rebecca Kai Dotlich. Reprinted by permission of Curtis Brown, Ltd.

"Bacteria" and "Skunks" by Joy Masoff from OH, YUCK! THE ENCYCLOPEDIA OF EVERYTHING NASTY. Copyright © 2000 by Joy Masoff. Reprinted by permission of Workman Publishing Co., Inc.

Cover design by Norma Ortiz; photographs by Ron Chapple/Taxi/Getty Images; Ryan McVay/PhotoDisc/Getty Images; Andy Sacks/Stone/Getty Images; interior design by Grafica

ISBN 0-439-04759-5

Table of Contents

Why Read Aloud?

by Janet Allen

I know that many of you who are reading this book have the same fond read-aloud memories that I have: someone we loved—or respected—reading us great stories filled with people who seemed more real than life, experiencing places and events we might never have imagined. In each of my adult moves, I've discarded clothing and furniture, dishes and knickknacks, but I have always managed to keep my 1945 set of *The Home University Bookshelf: Famous Stories and Verse* from which I was read to every day during my childhood.

I don't think my situation is unique. I seldom meet adults who tell me that what inspired their love of reading was a textbook. I often meet teachers who tell me of a special teacher, or parent or grandparent or aunt, who read aloud to them. They have tattered copies of *Charlotte's Web* and *The Little Engine That Could* that were somehow salvaged after multiple readings. As educators, I believe we have to ask ourselves: *What it is that makes that read-aloud time so significant in our development as readers*

Read Aloud Is Risk-Free

Read aloud has no risk for the listener. It does not discriminate. Proficient readers and struggling readers alike have equal access to the text. While there is a great deal of research supporting the importance of this strategy in early childhood development, I have come to believe that even our older students must go back and capture that magic in order to develop as self-motivated readers.

For struggling readers, read-aloud time provides the opportunity for students to give their full attention to enjoyment of language and the visual images that language creates for them while someone else does the processing of the text (decoding). For fluent readers, their worlds grow larger with each new word, character, situation, or event.

No Excuses!

While most of us probably don't need an excuse to read aloud, I am often asked why I place such emphasis on it—in teaching both children and adults. In response to that question, I created a list of reasons for reading aloud (see sidebar).

I think this list gives us sufficient justification if we need it. For me, the justification came from seeing the significant changes in my students' reading and writing attitudes and competencies, which I could tie directly to the reading aloud we did together. From Gary Paulsen's "Tuning" in *The Winter Room*, my students learned about sensory language; from Maya Angelou's "No Loser, No Weeper" in *Poems*, my students comprehended the story that is a poem; and from Dudley Randall's "Ballad of Birmingham" in his poetry collection *Black Poets*, my students vicariously lived the gut-wrenching, experience of the Sunday School bombing in Birmingham, Alabama, in 1963. Additionally, they learned the structure of stories, poems, news articles, speeches, and memoir. Read aloud formed the foundation for future writing-craft lessons, for discussion, for rethinking our choices and for making us laugh and cry, listen and think.

WHY USE READ ALOUDS?

Read alouds:

* expose students to a wide variety of literature.

* build content area background knowledge as well as general word knowledge.

* help students develop interests for later self-selection or reading materials.

* provide opportunities for assessing story development and characterization.

* facilitate students' abilities to compare and contrast.

* fine tune students' observational and listening skills.

* create an atmosphere for developing good discussion skills.

* develop higher level thinking skills.

* allow you to assess students' growth as listeners and thinkers.

* allow students to anticipate or predict.

* model effective reading behaviors.

* allow you to assess attention span and its increase over time.

* provide opportunities to share a love of books.

* create a community of learners and readers.

Preparing for Read Aloud

In *I Know Why the Caged Bird Sings*, Maya Angelou says, "Words mean more than what is set down on paper. It takes the human voice to infuse them with the shades of deeper meaning." If read aloud is so important and our voices are making a critical difference in the level of meaning-making, how do we get ready for it? Many teachers tell me of administrators who have come to their classrooms to do observations or evaluations but have turned around and left, preferring to return when the teachers are "really teaching." Part of the notion that read aloud is somehow "non-teaching" time may have arisen from our practice of reading aloud with "extra" time. But read aloud is important instructional time and as such needs to be prepared for in the same way we prepare for any significant teaching moment: preparing ourselves to do the read aloud; preparing our students for participating; and making sure the environment is conducive for reading, listening, and learning.

Teacher Preparation for Read-Aloud Choices

Teacher preparation for read aloud actually involves several steps. The first is choosing what to read. What texts you choose will depend on the interests, age, and needs of your students, as well as their reading and life experiences. Once you choose the text, there are several points of preparation that will make the read-aloud experience richer for both you and your students. After many years of reading aloud to students who were interested neither in school nor in reading, I've developed a keen sense of the strategies needed to grab the attention of even the most reluctant students and make them want to keep listening.

- Practice reading the text prior to reading with your students.
- Choose texts you enjoy reading.
- Choose places where you'd like to stop—in order to build suspense, clarify words, or help listeners who might be lost.
- Highlight words or situations that may need some explanation.
- Check for background information about the author, time period, illustrator, or text in case students' questions veer in that direction.
- Choose a consistent time for read aloud. Read aloud is an effective transition into and out of a class period. It is also effective for transitioning from one activity to another.
- Choose a time for read aloud that is as free from distractions as possible.
- Read the text with passion. Laugh and cry, wonder and question, so that students see an authentic response from you, the reader.
- If the read aloud is part of a larger unit or inquiry, be prepared to help students make the connection a conscious one.
- Provide time and opportunity for students to make connections to their lives.

Preparing Students and the Environment for Read Aloud

Preparing students for read aloud is more difficult the first few times you do than it is once students come to expect and demand read aloud sessions. Taking a proactive approach in this area of preparation will save you a lot of class time and gain a lot in terms of students' comprehension and response.

Establish clear expectations of student behavior during read aloud. If you want students to do nothing other than listen, that needs to be established with the first read aloud. If, however, you wish to allow students to doodle, create images, or take notes, establish parameters for those activities.

Be prepared to extend the read-aloud session. Keep chart paper, overhead transparencies, and markers available in case student discussion leads to memorable talk.

Responding to Read Aloud

Student responses to read aloud vary in much the same way that students' responses vary to any other classroom activity. Responses depend on a range of circumstances and interests. While doing observations in a classroom, I noted the following typical response patterns during and after the read alouds:

- sharing opinions about characters and motivations,
- noting language and mimicking, unique words, phrases, or sounds,
- stating pleasure/displeasure with situations or endings,
- making non-verbal responses (body language, intake of breath),
- comparing to other works of literature,
- commenting on physical characteristics of book (cover, illustrations, etc.),
- offering alternative versions of the text,
- asking questions and making judgments as text critics.

Responses to read aloud increase when you choose selections mindfully and read in ways that engage students as listeners, thinkers, and responders.

We hope that as you and your students share the read alouds we have compiled in this anthology you find the joy in reading and listening to them that we did in collecting and choosing them. Donald Graves says, "As I read, the children compose their own images, but the feelings they create together create a literate bond that is unique in human existence." It is our belief that these read alouds will lead you and your students to many other read alouds—and each day those read alouds will further connect the bond that forms your literate community.

STORY	GENRE	SYNOPSIS	RECOMMENDED NUMBER OF READ-ALOUD SESSIONS (20 minutes per session)
All the Cats in the World	Fiction	An elderly woman finds companionship and an unexpected friendship while caring for homeless cats.	1
The Elian Gonzalez Story	Nonfiction	The story of one of the most controversial political events of recent history.	1
There's a Cobra in the Bathroom	Poem	A humorous poem about a teacher's reluctance to believe an unlikely event.	1
The Triangle Shirtwaist Fire	Nonfiction	The story of the tragic factory fire that led to the establishment of fire safety laws.	1
A Mouthful	Fiction	A humorous short story about a practical joker who has the tables turned on him.	1
Sir Gawain and the Green Knight	Legend	This classic legend speaks to listeners about keeping your word.	1
The Escape	Fiction	A gripping and gnarly story that takes you through a prisoner's desperate attempt to escape prison—even if it means facing his worst fears.	1-2
Around the River Bend	Historical Fiction	A sister reflects upon her brother and the Vietnam War and learns a valuable lesson about forgiveness.	2-3
Breaking a Bad Habit	Trickster Tale	Habits are the hardest thing to break—whether you are human or not.	1
Bacteria: The Good, the Bad, and the Stinky	Nonfiction	Everything you need to know about bacteria.	1
New Kid	Fiction	When she changes schools, Emma learns that it is not easy to be the new kid.	2
The Tell-Tale Heart	Classic Fiction	A retelling of Edgar Allan Poe's classic tale of death and guilt.	1

Bandaids and Five Dollar Bills	Poem	This poem addresses social issues including AIDS and drug abuse.	1
Sick	Poem	A humorous poem about a kid campaigning for a day off from school.	1
9/11: An Eyewitness Account	Nonfiction	A woman's eyewitness account of one of the worst days in American history.	1
The Attack on Pearl Harbor	Historical Nonfiction	A vivid description about a catastrophic day in American history.	1
Only a Dollar's Worth	Fiction	Sometimes the most frugal people teach the most valuable lessons.	1-2
The Coal Mine Disaster	Nonfiction	A description of one of the worst mining disasters in recent history.	1
I Escaped a Violent Gang	Memoir	This powerful admission addresses the life-threatening difficulties of gang life.	1
Frozen Alive	Nonfiction	The bone-chilling true account of one young boy's miraculous escape from death.	1
Autobiography in Five Short Chapters	Poem	A poem about the change in one student's perspective on responsibility.	1
Roger's Swim	Nonfiction	Remarkable true recounting of an astonishing coincidence.	1
Testing New Waters	Poem	A poem about taking a chance.	1
Homework Poems	Poems	Funny poems about homework excuses.	1-3
The Plague	Historical Fiction	A devastating period of history comes alive when told through the eyes of a fictional boy.	4-5
The Birmingham Sunday School Bombing	Magazine Article	A magazine article about the Birmingham bombing.	1
The Ballad of Birmingham	Poem	A poem about the loss of a child in the Birmingham bombing.	1

All the Cats in the World

by Sonia Levitin

Do you know someone who feeds an animal that doesn't belong to him or her—like birds, or squirrels, or deer, or even stray cats? What do you think prompts—or causes—a person to do such an act?

In the story you are about to hear, you will meet a lonely old woman named Mikila. Yes, she is lonely, but there is one thing that brings Mikila comfort. Every day she climbs the rocks at the seashore to feed the cats. One day the lighthouse keeper begins to make fun of Mikila and her cat-feeding habit. Does she quit? Does she continue? You'll find out. And you'll also find out what valuable lesson Mikila learns.

Down by the seaside, among the rugged rocks and cliffs and in the shadow of an old lighthouse, lived many, many cats of different kinds and different colors. All were wild. They howled in the night.

Some had been left by thoughtless people. Others had strayed from their homes. Many had been born right at the water's edge, so this was the only home they had ever known.

Now, it happened that two old women, noticing the cats, began to feed them. Soon they came every morning, just after dawn, with sacks full of food—liver scraps, fish heads, and bread crusts. The two women, Nella and Mikila, were good friends. They were still quite nimble and strong. They would clamber down among the rocks, calling, making certain that every cat got its share.

"Ah, Mittens," Nella or Mikila would say, "Here is your breakfast. Good morn-ing, little Tabby, Tiger, and Freckles."

After each cat had eaten and licked its whiskers and paws, up the rocky path the women climbed, slower now and hot from the morning sun, talking as good friends do.

One day poor Nella died, and Mikila was left all alone. She wept bitterly. She went to the church to pray.

Late in the afternoon she remembered the cats. She had not fed the cats!

Weary and sad as she was, Mikila hurried to the fishmonger, the butcher, and the grocer, and for a few pennies she gathered the scraps for her cats.

She arrived at the cliffs, hot and out of breath. When the cats saw Mikila, they emerged from behind the rocks meowing, their tails held high. "Where were you?" they seemed to say reproachfully. "We were hungry. Why did you fail us?"

"I did not fail you, my little ones," Mikila said, as though they had really spoken. "Our friend, Nella, is no more on this Earth. But you will not go hungry, as long as there is a breath in Mikila's body."

Suddenly Mikila heard gruff laughter. She looked about, startled. Partway up the slope, on a long, flat rock, a bearded old man sat looking down at her.

"Woman!" he called. "What are you doing with that sack of food?"

"I'm feeding the cats!" shouted Mikila. "What does it look like to you?"

"It looks like a foolish woman," replied the man rudely, "meddling where she doesn't belong."

"I belong here as well as you!" retorted Mikila.

"I belong here well enough," called the man, "for I am the keeper of the lighthouse."

"Then keep your lighthouse," shouted Mikila, "and leave me alone!"

Still the old man watched. By and by he called down, more curious than rude, "Woman, pray tell me, are you so rich that you can afford to feed these filthy creatures?"

Mikila retorted, "I manage with a few pennies a day, buying leftovers from the shops. Is it any business of yours?"

Angrily she left, determined to bring even more scraps tomorrow. She would show that old man—what did she care that he thought her foolish?

The next day Mikila's sack was heavy as she went down to the sea, calling, "Tina, Bennie, and Spots! Here Tabby, Minnie, and Puff."

Again she heard harsh laughter from up on the ledge.

"Old woman!" the man called down. "Aren't you afraid, at your age, to climb those rocks? You could fall and break your legs!"

"I'm not afraid!" She laughed and thumbed her nose at him.

It rained the next day, and Mikila yearned to stay home. But the old man might think she was afraid, so she covered her head with a kerchief and went as usual to feed the cats.

This time the man was not there. But Mikila heard the deep bellow of the foghorn, and she saw the broad beam of light coming from the lighthouse. She knew he was tending to his job.

Just as Mikila finished, the old man appeared at the top of the ridge, followed by a pet goat. He did not come down, for the rocks were wet and slippery, but called out, "Old woman! How stubborn you are to come out even in this bitter weather! I have never seen such a one as you!"

"I am not stubborn, I am faithful!" Mikila shouted.

The old man shook his head, laughing, and disappeared inside the lighthouse.

Mikila walked away slowly, her feet sinking into the wet sand. Her clothes clung to her body, and she shivered. At home, a hot bath and a cup of tea did much to restore her spirits, but she felt very tired and began to sneeze.

The next morning Mikila's throat was sore. Her head hurt. Surely the cats could manage without her for just one day, she thought.

Then she remembered the old man's rude laughter and her talk about being faithful.

"One who is faithful does not give up so easily." She grunted and groaned all the way down to the shore.

As before, the old man sat upon the rock shelf, and when he saw Mikila, he called down, "Old woman, tell me one thing. *Why* do you feed these cats?"

"BECAUSE THEY ARE HUNGRY!" Mikila shouted.

"Hungry!" The man held his sides with laughter. "Hungry! Ha-ha-ha! That's a good one! Don't you know there are millions of hungry cats in the world? Can you feed all the cats in the world?"

Mikilia did not answer. Wearily she gathered up her empty sack and went home, weeping.

That night Mikila's bones ached. Even hot tea did not help. For three days and nights she lay sick with fever. The old man's words echoed in her head: "Woman, you are wasteful and stubborn and foolish." She thought, "It is true. I can never feed all the hungry cats in the world. I am tired and sick. Most of all, I am sick and tired of being taunted by the terrible old man. I will go no more to feed the cats." She lay in her bed grieving.

At last she slept deeply, and on the fourth morning she woke up feeling strong—not only strong, but determined; not only determined, but angry!

She got up in haste, pulled on her clothes, snatched up her sack, and hurried to gather food for the cats.

As she hustled, Mikila planned what she would tell that rude old man. *He* was the foolish one, the stubborn one, the stupid one. Couldn't he see what *he* did every day in his lighthouse was exactly the same as feeding the cats?

She could hardly wait to catch him on the ledge and shout up, "Why do you bother to send a beam from your light-house? You can't save every ship in the ocean. You can't guide them all safely to shore. Why do you even try?"

As Mikila picked her way down the rocky path, she called, "Come, Tiger, Mittens, Freckles, Puff. Oh, my poor little ones. Mikila is here."

She expected to see the cats shivering, half dead from hunger. But instead they leaped nimbly out, playfully rubbing against her legs.

"Ah, my dear ones," Mikila exclaimed, "how I have missed you! But—you look well fed. How can it be?"

Now Mikila saw the old man's goat licking salt from the rocks, and in the next moment there was the old man himself. He stood bent toward the shyest of the cats, feeding it from a sack of scraps.

"What are you doing?" cried Mikila in surprise.

He turned and stammered, "I—why—I—what does it look like to you, old woman?"

Mikila stared at him until his face grew very red and he looked away out to sea.

"Are you so rich," she taunted, "that you have money to waste on these filthy creatures?"

The old man shuffled his feet.

Mikila folded her arms and asked, "Why do you come out in this bitter weather? What a foolish man you are!"

The old man smiled slyly while the cats milled about his feet. "Actually," he said, "It was not my idea."

"Then whose?" asked Mikila, tapping her foot.

"My goat's. Ulysses'. He dragged me down here. What else could I do?"

"You could have stayed in your light-house," said Mikila.

"But Ulysses is very stubborn," replied the man. "He is also strong and clever. In fact," said the man with a grin, "he is in many ways like you."

"Like me?" Mikila tossed her head. "Many thanks for comparing me to a goat!"

"But this goat," said the man earnestly, "is my good friend." He patted the goat's head, with its stubby horns and stiff hair. "We have many conversations."

"Then Ulysses must have told you," said Mikila dryly, "that you cannot possibly feed all the cats in the world."

The old man grinned broadly, and his face creased into a thousand wrinkles. "Of course," he replied. "We all know that. But I can at least feed these close at hand. It is much the same," he added, "as tending the lighthouse."

Mikila was silent for a long moment. Then she smiled. "Since Ulysses cares so much about the cats," she said, "send him to me tomorrow. I will show him which shops sell the very best scraps."

"A fine idea," exclaimed the old man. "But Ulysses goes nowhere without me. We shall come together." He turned and, imitating Mikila's own high voice, said, "Good-bye now, Roscoe, Tiger, and Puff. See you tomorrow!"

And so, each day after that, the man and the woman and the goat went together to buy the scraps and feed the cats—not all the cats in the world, but the ones that lived among the rocks in the shadow of the old lighthouse. You can see the three of them walking up the rocky path together, talking and laughing as good friends do.

READER'S TIP

An interesting discussion following this read aloud is on *character* and *setting*. You can begin this discussion with questions such as these:

✳ As I read this story, what images did you picture in your mind?
✳ Do you know people like Mikila and the lighthouse keeper?
✳ Was Mikila doing a good thing or a silly thing?

The Elian Gonzalez Story

by Michael Dahlie

"Little Havana" is a Cuban neighborhood in Miami, Florida. It is a peaceful community that rarely sees any trouble. In the spring of 2000, however, the community was turned upside down. Huge crowds gathered in the streets. Police officers set up roadblocks. Helicopters circled the skies. Hundreds of television and newspaper reporters roamed the area. What was the cause of all this excitement? Was it a hurricane? A bomb threat? No. The cause of the excitement was a six-year-old boy. He had been found floating in the ocean four months earlier. And ever since his rescue, his story had been causing an uproar in Little Havana—and throughout the rest of the world. Why were so many people interested in his story? Let's find out.

It all started in November 1999. It was Thanksgiving Day. Two men were fishing off the coast of Florida. Suddenly, the men spotted something strange in the distance. They could make out an inner tube, but something seemed to be strapped to it. They weren't sure what it was. After they got closer, they decided it was nothing. They thought it was just a rag doll. But then they saw its hand move and realized it was a little boy.

Quickly, they dived in to save him. When they pulled the boy onto the boat, he was shivering and asking for water. He had not had anything to drink for days.

The fishermen rushed the boy to the hospital. He was badly sunburned and barely alive. But it looked like he was going to make it. The doctors called it a miracle. The fishermen who saved him were overjoyed. It was a short celebration, however. Soon they began to piece together the story of how the boy had ended up on the inner tube.

The boy's name was Elian Gonzalez. Four days earlier, he and his mother had set out for Florida from a beach in Cuba. Elian's mother and father were divorced, and his mother wanted to start a new life in the United States. She knew the boy and his father would miss each other. But she thought Elian would be better off in the U.S. Under Castro—Cuba's leader—people have few freedoms. And most Cubans are very poor.

Eleven other people were crowded in the boat with Elian and his mom. They all knew the journey would be dangerous. It was 90 miles across rough, shark-infested waters. And the boat they were traveling on was homemade and flimsy. But they were willing to risk it. They were determined to leave Cuba.

On the second night of their journey, a storm blew in. The small boat couldn't handle the huge waves and heavy winds. Before long, the boat turned over. It sank. And it took six passengers with it.

There were only two inner tubes to hold the rest of the passengers. A man and a woman took one, Elian, his mother, and three other people grabbed hold of the other. Elian was strapped to the top of the inner tube. The rest of the refugees held on to the sides. But it soon became too hard to hold on. One-by-one the ocean took their lives. Poor Elian watched as his own mother slipped beneath the ocean's surface and drowned. The next people he would see would be the fishermen who saved him.

The news of Elian's story sent shock waves through Florida's large Cuban community. Elian's American relatives were told of the tragedy. Soon his great-uncle went to the hospital. He took Elian back to his house in Little Havana. The boy was safe but scared. He wondered what was going to happen to him. Would he stay in the U.S.? Or would he return to Cuba to be with his father again?

In other cases, it would be a simple decision. Most people would say that a boy who loses his mother should live with his father. But since Castro's communist government took control of Cuba forty years ago, Cuba and the U.S. have been enemies. The U.S. says that Castro's government mistreats its people and that Cubans are not free. And Elian's American family agrees. The family said Cuba is a terrible place for a boy to grow up. They said it would be wrong to send Elian back to Cuba. He would have no money and none of the freedoms people in the U.S. have.

But Elian's father thought differently. When he heard that his son was alive, he demanded that Elian be returned to Cuba. Elian's father said that it was wrong for a boy to grow up without his parents. He said Elian belonged with him—his father. Cuban President Fidel Castro and his government quickly took the father's side. A major showdown was beginning to brew.

✳

Soon, people in both Cuba and the United States were talking about Elian. What might have been just an argument between family members became an argument between nations. Huge protests were held in Cuba. People were demanding Elian's return. Castro even sent Elian's grandfather and father to Washington, D.C., to bring Elian back in person.

Protests were also held in Little Havana. People began to surround the house of Elian's uncle. They stayed near the house day and night. Everyone was saying that Elian should remain in the U.S. They held posters with Elian's picture. They chanted and sang and prayed. And they spent the nights in tents set up on the streets. Police officers and reporters were everywhere. Politicians showed up. Even celebrities like singer Gloria Estefan joined in. The protesters were determined to keep Elian in the U.S.

The protests in Cuba and Miami lasted for months. No one was willing to give in. But the fact was that neither group had the power to decide Elian's future. In the end, it was up to the United States Government and the Attorney General, Janet Reno, to make the decision.

Working with several lawyers, Janet Reno carefully looked at the facts of the case. She weighed both sides of the problem and considered Elian's needs. Eventually she made a choice. She decided that the boy should go back to Cuba. She agreed that it would be good for Elian to grow up in the United States. But she thought it was more important for Elian and his father to be together.

Elian's father was thrilled. He was in Washington D.C. and anxious to see his son. But Elian's American relatives were furious. They understood why the boy should be with his father. But they didn't want Elian to go back to Cuba. Elian was living with them, and they wanted it to stay that way. They told Janet Reno that they didn't want to nor would they give the boy up.

Janet Reno stood firm. She listened to the family's concerns, but she said that the boy must be returned. She said that it was wrong for Elian and his father to be apart any longer. Still, the family delayed handing the boy over.

So Reno took action. In the early morning hours of April 22, 2000, she sent armed U.S. officials to the home of Elian's American relatives. They burst into the house and took Elian by force. The protesters outside were angry. The relatives did not want to let Elian go. But none of them had any choice. Soon Elian was on a plane. Within hours, he was with his father in Washington D.C. They had been separated for five months.

In the days that followed, many people were upset with Reno's actions.

Newspapers printed pictures of armed men taking a crying Elian from his relatives. People wondered if Reno had used too much force. But Reno defended her decision. She said it was a show of force, not the use of force. She pointed out that because of this show of force, no one was hurt. She also repeated that it was important that the boy be returned to his father immediately. It could not have waited any longer. Action was necessary.

But there were more pictures than the ones of the armed U.S. officials taking Elian. Newspapers also printed photographs of the reunion between Elian and his father. From the pictures, no one could doubt how happy the two were together. And all the eyewitness reports said the same thing. Elian and his father were overjoyed to see one another. Elian's father was laughing and crying, and so was Elian.

Today people are still debating Elian's case. This six-year-old boy nearly died, and he watched his own mother drown. He's been through a lot. It will be hard for him to get over his pain. People want to make sure he gets the help he needs.

Some people say Janet Reno's decision to send Elian back to Cuba with his father was a bad one. They say it will hurt him. Other people say the decision will help. But in the end, it's too early to say. Only time will tell. For now, most people agree that the best thing for Elian is to live as much of a normal life as possible. Hopefully, being with his father is at least a step in that direction.

There's a Cobra in the Bathroom

by Kalli Dakos

Teachers can hear some pretty far-fetched, over-the-top stories from students. Wouldn't you agree? As you listen to this poem, ask yourself, "Would I have believed it?"

There's a cobra in the bathroom, Mrs. Kay.

What did you say?

There's a cobra in the bathroom, Mrs. Kay,
And he won't go away!

Sandra, nine times five is forty-five,
Rick, check your spelling.
A cobra in the bathroom, Renee?
Why don't you clean it away?

*I can't **touch** him, Mrs. Kay,*
I'm too scared to even blink.
I have goosebumps everywhere, and
Now he's crawling on the sink.

Robert, eight times five is not thirty-five,
Mary, please stop talking,
Our spelling test is Friday.
Did that cobra go away?

No, Mrs. Kay, I see him
Slithering on the floor,
And I don't want to stay here
Even one second more.

Jim, put the gum in the garbage,
Joe, your work's so neat.
Please sit at your desk, Renée,
This is not the time to play.

I can't move, Mrs. Kay,
He's quite dangerous, you see,
And if I even budge an inch,
He'll spread his poison over me.

Class, line up for music,
John, pick up your shoes.
You look scared to death, Renée,
I'll check that bathroom now, okay?

(Slam!)

AH! AH! AH! AH!
THERE'S ... A ... COBRA ... IN ... THERE ... !

I told you, Mrs. Kay,
That he wouldn't go away.

READER'S TIP

* The lines that are written in italics are the lines of one student. All of the other lines are those of the teacher as she manages the whole class.

* As you read the line "Ah! Ah! Ah! Ah!" you may wish to scream loudly. The effect will be powerful!

The Triangle Shirtwaist Fire

by Harrison Powers

If you were to work in an office building today, it wouldn't be unusual to have frequent fire drills—just like you do in school. And it wouldn't be unusual for a fire marshal to walk through the office floors making sure that there was not too much trash cluttering the halls. The marshal would also check to see that fire and emergency exits were kept clear.

Sadly, fire safety has not always been so carefully practiced and observed. In fact, many years ago in a factory in the middle of New York City, fire safety was not practiced at all.

It was 4:30 on a sunny Saturday afternoon. At the Triangle Shirtwaist Company, the work week was almost over. Five hundred workers finished up their chores. Most of them were women and young girls. They made the blouses, called "shirtwaists," that the company sold.

The Triangle Company had the top three floors of a ten-story building. The building was one of New York's early "high-rises." Built of brick and stone, it was said to be fireproof. But inside, it was framed with wood. Bolts of cloth lined the walls. Piles of rags and tissue paper littered the work area. The sewing machines and the floors were soaked with oil.

Two narrow stairways led down to the street. The door to one was kept locked. A passageway only twenty inches wide led to the other. There was only one fire escape. And it stopped at the second floor.

The year before, the owners had been warned. The building was a firetrap. But no changes were ever made. No fire doors were installed. No sprinklers were installed. The workers never even had a fire drill. On March 25, 1911, fate finally caught up with them.

A guard stood at the door to the stairway. His job was to check each woman's purse as she left. The owners were afraid the women might steal scraps of fabric. They were lined up, ready to file out. Then, a young woman ran to her boss. "There's a fire, Mr. Bernstein!"

It wasn't the first fire in the shop. There had been other small fires. The last one had been two weeks ago.

Now, the men sprang into action. But this time, the fire got away from them. They threw pails of water on it. But the water only seemed to spread the flames.

The manager called off his men. "You can't do anything here. Try to get the women out!"

Screams of "*Fire!*" filled the eighth floor. Workers jammed the narrow exit. Later, firemen found their bodies piled up at the door.

One woman tried to warn the others above. A teletype machine connected with the tenth floor. The fire raged around her. But she sat down and started typing. A clerk on the tenth floor took the message. "The place is on fire," it read. "Run for your lives."

They thought it was a joke. But within minutes, the fire came in through the windows.

On the ninth floor, they had no warning a all.

There were two freight elevators. The frantic workers crowded in. The elevator cars started down. One never made it. The people left behind jumped down the shaft. They landed on top of the car. More followed. They jammed the elevator so it wouldn't move. Afterwards, nineteen bodies were found wedged into the shaft.

On the street below, a crowd was gathering. At 4:45 P.M., the fire trucks had arrived. But there was little the firemen could do. Their ladders only reached as high as the fifth floor.

The women started jumping. They smashed the windows with their fists. The first woman climbed out on the ledge. Her hair, streaming down her back, was ablaze. She held out her arms, as if sleepwalking, and stepped off. From different windows, three more followed. In all, forty-six women jumped to their deaths. Some of them held hands in a group-jump.

Firemen held out their nets. But the force of the falling bodies was too great for them. Every net ripped to shreds.

Some workers on the tenth floor made it to the roof. Hundreds of others escaped as well. They were the lucky ones.

That evening, the charred remains of many bodies were taken out. The victims were placed in coffins. The coffins were lined up—one hundred and forty-six.

The news spread. Thousands came looking for loved ones. They filed past the coffins. Mothers found daughters. Sisters found sisters. Husbands found wives. Their screams filled the night.

Seven bodies were never identified. They were too badly burned.

The next day, firemen picked through the rubble. They found fourteen engagement rings. Fourteen weddings never took place that spring.

All over New York City and all around the country, too, sorrow at the tragedy was followed by anger and outrage that it had been allowed to happen. The new garment workers' union now found public opinion behind its fight to improve working conditions.

Fire laws, too, were strengthened. Buildings were to have enough fire exits. Regular inspections made sure that exits were kept free and the fire extinguishers were working. Materials that might catch fire were no longer allowed to pile up in aisles. Fire drills became part of the routine. Not all fires can be prevented, but everything has been done to make sure there will never be another disaster like the Triangle Shirtwaist Fire.

A Mouthful

by Paul Jennings

Some stories make you laugh because they are just really funny. Others make you laugh because you identify with the situations that the main character has gotten him- or herself in. And then . . . there are stories that are just plain gross. Hilariously gross! See what makes this story funny to you.

Parents are embarrassing. Take my dad. Every time a friend comes to stay the night, he does something that makes my face go red. Now don't get me wrong. He is a terrific dad. I love him but sometimes I think he will never grow up.

He loves playing practical jokes.

This behavior first started the night Anna came to sleep over.

Unknown to me, Dad sneaks into my room and puts Doona, our cat, on the spare bed. Doona loves sleeping on beds. What cat doesn't?

Next Dad unwraps a little package that he has bought at the magic shop.

Do you know what is in it? Can you believe this? It is a little piece of brown plastic cat poo. Pretend cat poo. Anyway he puts this piece of cat poo on Anna's pillow and pulls up the blankets. Then he tiptoes out and closes the door.

I do not know any of this is happening. Anna and I are sitting up late watching videos. We eat chips covered in sauce and drink two whole bottles of Diet Coke.

Finally we decided to go to bed. Anna takes ages and ages cleaning her teeth. She is one of those kids who is into health. She has a thing about germs. She always places paper on the toilet seat before she sits down. She is so clean.

Anyway, she puts on her tracksuit bottoms and gets ready for bed. Then she pulls back the blankets. Suddenly she sees the bit of cat's poo. "Ooh, ooh, ooh," she screams. "Oh, look, disgusting. Foul. Look what the cat's done on my pillow."

Suddenly Dad bursts into the room. "What's up, girls?" he says with a silly grin on his face. "What's all the fuss about?"

Anna is pulling a terrible face. "Look," she says in horror as she points at the pillow.

Dad goes over and examines the plastic poo. "Don't let a little thing like that worry you," he says. He picks up the plastic poo and pops it into his mouth. He gives a grin. "D'licioush," he says through closed lips.

"Aargh," screams Anna. She rushes over to the window and throws up chips, sauce, and Diet Coke. Then she looks at Dad in disgust.

Dad is a bit taken aback at Anna being sick. "It's okay," he says, taking the plastic poo out of his mouth. "It's not real." Dad gives a laugh and off he goes. And off goes Anna. She decides that she wants to go home to her own house. And I don't blame her.

"Dad," I yell after Anna is gone. "I am never speaking to you again."

"Don't be such a baby," he says. "It's only a little joke."

It's always the same. Whenever a friend comes over to stay, Dad plays practical jokes. We have fake hands in the trash, exploding drinks, pepper in the food, short-sheeted beds, and Dracula's blood seeping out of Dad's mouth. Some of the kids think it's great. They wish their dads were like mine.

But I hate it. I just wish he was normal.

He plays tricks on Bianca.

And Yasmin.

And Nga.

And Karla.

None of them go home like Anna. But each time I am so embarrassed.

And now I am worried.

Cynthia is coming to stay. She is the school captain. She is beautiful. She is smart. Everyone wants to be her friend. And now she's sleeping over at our house.

"Dad," I say. "No practical jokes. Cynthia is very mature. Her father would never play practical jokes. She might not understand."

"No worries," says Dad.

Cynthia arrives, but we do not watch videos. We slave away on our English homework. We plan our speeches for the debate in the morning. We go over our parts in the school play. After all that, we go out and practice shooting baskets, because Cynthia is captain of the basketball team. Every now and then I pop into the bedroom to check for practical jokes. It is best to be on the safe side.

We also do the dishes because Cynthia offers—yes—offers to do it.

Finally it is time for bed. Cynthia changes into her nightie in the bathroom and then joins me in the bedroom. "The cat's on my bed," she says. "But it doesn't matter. I like cats." She pulls back the blankets.

And screams. "Aagh. Cat poo. Filthy cat poo on my pillow." She yells and yells and yells.

Just then Dad bursts into the room with a silly grin on his face. He goes over and looks at the brown object on the pillow. "Don't let a little thing like that worry you," he says. He picks it up and pops it into his mouth. But this time he does not give a grin. His face freezes over.

"Are you looking for this?" I say.

I hold up the bit of plastic poo that Dad had hidden under the blankets earlier that night.

Dad looks at the cat.

Then he rushes over to the window and is sick.

Cynthia and I laugh like mad.

We do love a good joke.

Ask students if this read aloud reminded them of a good joke that they played on someone . . . or that was played on them!

Sir Gawain and the Green Knight

A Retelling of a Classic King Arthur Legend

Many old legends exist about King Arthur and his Knights of the Round Table. These legends have been used over the years to tell about traits that we—as good people—strive to attain. Traits like honesty, courage, and loyalty. In this legend, "Sir Gawain and the Green Knight," you'll see how of one of King Arthur's finest knights faces the ultimate test of bravery.

What is the message of this legend? What does it teach us about bravery? You decide.

ld legends tell us that more than 1,000 years ago England had a king named Arthur. King Arthur had a group of brave knights. They were known as the Knights of the Round Table.

Every Christmas, the Knights of the Round Table came together. They feasted on rich foods. And they told about their adventures. Year after year this ritual took place. One year, however, during their feast, something extraordinary happened.

The Knights of the Round Table were laughing and telling stories when all of a sudden the palace's heavy door swung open.

In the doorway, mounted on a huge horse, was a green knight. Everything about him was green: his face, his armor, even his horse; and he carried a massive green ax.

"Which of you is King Arthur?" he asked.

The king stood up. "I am Arthur," he said.

"I have heard that your knights are the bravest in the world," said the Green Knight. "I want to know which of them is brave enough to do what I ask."

"Any knight here is brave enough," King Arthur said. "What is it that you ask?"

The Green Knight got off his horse, cleared his throat, held up his ax, and then spoke. "I want a knight to take this ax and strike me with it."

The room was silent.

"Are you all cowards?" he roared.

King Arthur spoke, "Sir, what you ask for makes no sense. You ask for your own death."

The Green Knight laughed loud and long.

A knight named Sir Gawain stepped forward. Gawain said, "No one laughs at the Knights of the Round Table. Hand me that ax, and I will strike your laughing head from your body!"

Gawain took the ax from the Green Knight and got ready to swing. "Just a minute," the Green Knight said. "This has to be fair. In return for striking me, I have the right to strike you back."

"You have the right, yes," said Gawain. "But, I must tell you, no man has ever survived a blow from me."

"We shall see," said the Green Knight. "You must promise that after you strike me tonight, you will come to my castle a year from now. Then, I will hold the ax and I will strike you with it."

Sir Gawain smiled, knowing that day would never come. "It will be as you wish. I promise," he said.

The Green Knight lifted his long green hair to expose his green neck. Gawain swung the ax and struck the Green Knight's neck, cutting his head clear off his body. The Green Knight's head bounced and rolled on the floor.

Oddly, the Green Knight's body did not fall. With his arms, he simply reached down and picked up his own rolling head by its green hair.

The Green Knight held his head in front of him. His lips smiled a cruel smile as the Green Knight started to speak. "Do not forget your promise, oh brave Knight. In one year, at my Green Castle in the North Country, meet me, and accept your fate."

And without looking back, the Green Knight, carrying his own head walked out the door.

A strange event? Absolutely. But in these times many strange events take place. So a year later Sir Gawain kept his promise.

Sir Gawain led his horse through the snow in the North Country until he found a castle. The lord of the castle, Lord Westall, helped Gawain into a chair by a warm fire. Lady Westall sat nearby.

Gawain asked Lord Westall about the Green Castle. "It is just an hour from here," Lord Westall said. "But they say a monster, some sort of Green Knight, kills everyone who goes near it."

Sir Gawain told the lord and lady about the promise he'd made to the Green Knight. "Are you sure you want to do this?" Lord Westall asked.

Gawain nodded. "I made a promise," he said.

"Very well. Sleep here tonight," the lord said.

The next morning, Lady Westall walked into Sir Gawain's room and woke him. "You must escape right now," she whispered. "I will help you."

"Thank you, but I have never broken a promise," Sir Gawain said.

"I can not let this happen to you. Run for your life!" the lady pleaded. "You're going to die!"

"No, I must go to the Green Castle," he said.

And that's exactly what he did.

Sir Gawain rode to the Green Castle and shouted at its walls: "Green Knight, I have come to keep my promise!"

The door opened. Out stepped the Green Knight. He held the ax. "Are you ready?" he asked.

Gawain didn't have time to answer. The Green Knight was already swinging the ax. Gawain closed his eyes. The Green Knight struck.

Gawain blinked. "What happened?" he wondered. "Am I still alive?" He turned his head from side to side. He felt his neck. The ax had stopped just as it cut the skin!

"Gawain, you have passed every test of a man who calls himself a knight," said the Green Knight. "Take a closer look at me. Do you know who I am?"

"That's right. I'm your host from last night," said the Green Knight. "I have put you through every test of bravery. You were brave in the face of death. You kept your promise, even when my wife wanted you to run away."

"But why? Who are you?" asked Sir Gawain.

"Ask not who I am, Sir Gawain," said the Green Knight. "Ask not why my skin is now green. Know only that I am the Green Knight—sent to test you, the bravest knight who clearly has no equal."

The Escape

by J.B. Stamper

Do you know what a phobia is? A phobia is a fear of something. Some people are afraid of heights. Some people are afraid of spiders. Some people are even afraid of the dark. In this story you are about to hear, you are going to meet a man named Boris. Boris is in prison and he has a couple of phobias. He's deathly afraid of rats. And he really hates tight, small, cramped spaces. Nothing bothers him more. As you listen to this tale, can you identify with Boris and his phobias?

Boris looked down the long, dark hallway of the prison. It looked endless.

He was being taken to a place that few people had seen. But everyone feared it. Solitary. The other prisoners said the word with a shudder.

Behind him, the guard laughed. "Well, this will teach you a lesson," he said. "Once you've been in solitary, there will be no more bad behavior from you."

Boris forced his feet to move down the hall. He knew there was no hope for him.

Seven years ago, he had committed a crime. It was a crime so terrible that even he could not believe that he had done it.

Now he was in prison for the rest of his life. He was trapped like an animal in a cage. He could not face it any longer!

That's why he had tried to escape.

It had been just after sunset. He was all alone in the courtyard. The guard who was supposed to be there had made a mistake. He had left Boris alone.

Boris had run for the wall like an animal. He had climbed up and was almost over. Then he had heard the words, "Freeze, prisoner!"

And he had frozen.

That was just yesterday. Now he was headed to an even worse cage.

"You don't have to put me in solitary," Boris said to the guard in a scared voice. "I'll never try that again. I promise!"

The guard just laughed. "You'll learn your lesson," he said again. "Maybe they'll let you out after a few months. But you're a tough one. I know what you did to get inside. You don't deserve anybody's pity."

Boris felt hopeless. It was no good trying. He would just have to deal with it, somehow.

They were coming to the end of the hallway. Boris saw the door at the end. He saw the bars across the small window in the door.

He knew that this was it. The others had told him what it would be like inside.

They were right. The guard unlocked three locks. Then he swung open the door. He pushed Boris inside.

The room was like a pen. It was long

and narrow with one bed. High up there was a small window with bars across it.

The walls were of old, rough stone. To Boris, it felt as if they were closing in on him.

His breath started to come in short gasps. His heart pounded. Boris turned to the guard.

"No," he begged. "I can't take it here. Let me go back to where I was. I'll never do anything wrong again."

"You should have thought of that earlier," the guard said. Then he slammed the heavy door in Boris's face.

Boris reached for the door. He grabbed the bars in his hands and tried to shake them.

"You'll be sorry!" he yelled after the guard.

The guard just looked back and laughed.

Boris sat down on the bed. He shut his eyes. He didn't want to look around the cell. He was afraid that he would lose his mind.

Thunder woke Boris from a terrible nightmare. In the nightmare, rats were running at him, screeching.

He opened his eyes. He was afraid the rats were really there. He hated rats more than anything. It was his biggest worry . . . that there might be rats in solitary.

Boris looked around the cell. It was almost dark. Then a flash of lightning lit up the cell. The light fell on the wall at the head of his bed.

In those few seconds of light, Boris saw something that made his heart leap. One of the stones in the wall looked different. There was a thin crack in the cement around it.

Boris tried to fight off a new feeling of hope. But he couldn't help himself.

※

Maybe another prisoner had dug around the rock. No one could see the crack unless they were lying on the bed. He had only seen it because of the lightning.

His hands were shaking. He reached down and grabbed the large stone. He moved it back and forth.

Then, suddenly, it came loose! Boris pulled, and the rock fell forward into his hands.

As Boris stared into the hole left by the rock, a flash of lightning lit it up. A tunnel stretched before him . . . with a rat hurrying down into it.

Boris jumped back in horror when he saw the rat. He thought about putting the large stone back in place.

Then another flash of lightning cut through the darkness of the cell. The tunnel lit up in front of him. It seemed to welcome him to freedom.

Boris measured the size of the tunnel with his eyes. It was narrow at the beginning. But then it became wider. It looked wide enough for him to crawl though.

Another flash of lightning lit up the tunnel. He searched for any sign of the rat.

"Maybe I didn't see it at all," Boris whispered to himself. "Maybe it was just a shadow of my nightmare."

Boris peered into the tunnel. He saw no sign of the rat. But his eyes fell on something else. There was a scrap piece of paper lying on the tunnel floor, near the entrance.

He reached in and pulled it out. He felt its dry surface. The paper was wrinkled with age.

He waited impatiently for the lightning

to light up the cell again. When it did, he quickly read the message on the paper.

"To the next prisoner who finds this paper," Boris read. "I escaped the horror of this cell by this passage. May you share my good luck."

The light faded away before Boris could finish reading the message. He sat in the darkness, shaking with fear and hope.

The message seemed to be written in a dark red liquid. He guessed that it was the blood of the person who had written it.

At last, the lightning came again. He read on, "This is the only way out!" The message was signed with two initials, "N.G."

Just then, Boris heard the guard's footsteps outside his cell. He threw himself over the stone and hole. He pressed his body against the wall.

He waited as the footsteps came to a stop outside his cell. He thought he would scream from the horrible tension.

Then the footsteps moved away. They slowly drifted down the hallway. Finally, the noise faded into the night.

Suddenly, Boris knew he could not wait any longer. He stuck his head into the tunnel and pushed the rest of his body through.

He tried to look back, but the tunnel was too narrow. There was no turning back now.

Boris squirmed deeper and deeper into the tunnel. Crawling on his stomach, he felt like a snake slithering into its hole. He felt the tunnel grow damper and colder.

Just as the tunnel began to grow slimy, it opened up and became wider.

Boris stood up on his trembling legs. He tried to see into the darkness ahead.

He put his hands out in front of him and walked slowly through the black tunnel.

The rocky walls were sharp and tore at his hands. He wiped the sweat from his forehead with one hand and felt warm blood oozing from it.

Boris felt sick. His legs became weak with fear. He dropped to his knees and fell forward onto his hands. Then he felt tiny, clawed feet run over his fingers.

Boris heard his own scream echo and echo through the tunnel.

Once again, the tiny claws of a rat dug into his hands. Boris jumped to his feet, hitting his head on the low ceiling of the tunnel.

Then he felt them all around him. The rats were running over his shoes. They were crawling at his legs.

Boris opened his mouth to scream. But he knew he had to be quiet. He dug a fist into his mouth. He made himself move forward into the tunnel.

All he could hope was the rats would not climb up his leg. If they did, he knew he would lose his mind.

Suddenly, the tunnel sloped down at a sharp angle. Boris's feet slipped forward. He landed on his back. He slid deeper and deeper into the tunnel. He no longer felt the rats around him. He no longer heard their claws scratching the rock.

Boris came to a stop where the floor of the tunnel suddenly became flat. His breath was coming in short gasps that tore at his lungs.

He picked himself up. He reached for the slimy walls of the tunnel that he had just fallen down.

Then the truth hit him like a blow. He could never go back. The walls of the tunnel behind him were too steep and slippery.

He had only one chance. He had to push on. He had to push on . . . and hope that there was an end to the tunnel.

Boris moved himself forward. He clawed at the walls with his hands, trying to hurry.

The tunnel was beginning to feel more and more narrow. His breath was coming in shorter and shorter gasps. Then the tunnel made a sharp turn to the left. Suddenly Boris saw something that made him cry out in relief. Through an opening in the distance, he could see the pale rays of the moon.

He was almost there. He could smell the night air. Boris struggled toward the patch of moonlight ahead of him.

The tunnel was turning upward. Boris had to grab both sides of the wall and dig his feet into the cracks in the wall. Slowly, he pulled himself up. Boris felt the blood from his cuts run down into his sleeves.

But the pain didn't matter. All that mattered was the patch of light ahead. Boris felt the night air against his face. He was close now. Close to freedom.

Then a sound behind him terrified him. It was the sound of those clawed feet. They were following him.

Boris scrambled up to the top of the tunnel even faster. The moonlight was so bright now that he could see his hands in front of him. He felt a rat brush against his leg. But he had only a few yards to go.

With his last bit of strength, Boris lunged toward the light. He felt his head crash into something hard and cold. For a moment he was stunned.

Then he opened his eyes. In front of him, the moon shone through the bars of a heavy gate. Still pressed up against it were the cold, white bones . . . of a skeleton.

There was no escape. There was no going back. This was it. Just Boris . . . and the rats.

Around the River Bend

by Sherry Garland

This story is set in 1969, at the height of the Vietnam War. The war took place far away in Southeast Asia. At the time, the United States was helping South Vietnam fight against North Vietnam. The North Vietnamese were Communists. The United States was against Communism. Many Americans, and many more Vietnamese, died during this war.

As this story begins, the main character is still dealing with the loss of her older brother, who had been killed a year before in Vietnam. She is camping with her parents along the banks of the Brazos River in Texas. During the night, she hears sounds of helicopters from a nearby army camp. Soldiers from the U.S. and South Vietnam are training at the camp. Those sounds make her think of Vietnam—and the war that claimed her brother.

As you listen to this story, see if you can understand how the main character is feeling. See if you can understand *why* and *how* her feelings may have changed by the end of the story.

The helicopters would not let me sleep. At first I only heard a distant hum, no louder than the buzz of a hornet. Then, one by one, the silhouettes appeared over the top of the cedar-covered mountains. They moved across the face of the moon in formation like fat dragonflies with blinking red eyes. The hum turned into loud chop-chop-chops that echoed throughout the river canyon where we camped. The choppers performed maneuvers, following the leader like squatty black geese on a southward migration.

Chill-bumps rose on my neck at the sight of the flying machines. I knew that American soldiers from nearby Camp Wolters rode inside them, training for combat. The terrain in this part of Texas, steep hills thick with trees and shrubs, was similar to Vietnam. *Vietnam*—the very word nauseated me. How many of those men in the choppers would never come back? I wondered. How many of them would end up like my brother, Larry?

I tried not to think of the last time I had seen Larry. A red-white-and-blue flag covered his closed casket. It was all the family had to look at during the chaplain's eulogy, during the hollow bugle notes playing taps, and the seven rifles firing three short bursts in salute. And not seeing Larry for a final farewell made it so much worse.

I got up from my bedroll and walked beside the river. It had been a year since

Larry's funeral and I thought I had put it out of my mind in the excitement of getting ready for school to start. But now the whirl of blades reminded me of the war on the other side of the world. My heart grew sick, thinking of the waste of so many lives. And for what? For some country that I had never heard of? Who cared what happened to them?

By the time I returned to the dew-soaked bedroll, it was midnight. Hour after hour the helicopter formations crept over the mountains. It was four o'clock and even the croaking frogs and crickets and my yapping dog, Frisky, had quieted when the maneuvers stopped.

The sun was high when I awoke. By the river, my father merrily skinned and gutted freshly caught fish. From under a live oak tree, I heard the familiar sound of crunching ice and saw my mother cranking homemade ice cream. Vanilla with peaches—Larry's favorite.

This September camping trip was an end-of-summer ritual in our family. But it just didn't feel right doing things like this without Larry. Didn't all this dredge up painful memories for my parents? I know it did for me.

"I can't believe you're making Larry's favorite ice cream," I said. My voice was as chilly as the September night had been. "It's like you and Daddy are trying to forget Larry. You're pretending he never existed."

"Honey, I know you miss him," she said softly. "Your father and I do too. But you can't stop living."

I grabbed my fishing rod and announced: "I'm going up the river." As I stomped along the narrow trail surrounded by wild flowers, weeds, and willow trees, a rabbit jumped from a patch of

purple thistles. Our dog Frisky charged after it and disappeared. A few moments later I heard her frantic yapping.

"Frisky!" I shouted, then whistled and slapped my thigh, hoping it wasn't a skunk. Or a rattlesnake. *You never know what's around the river bend*, Larry used to always say with an optimistic smile. He even said it the night he packed his suitcase for boot camp. "You never know what's around the river bend, kid," he had said to me. And that was the last time I saw him.

As I rounded the bend, I saw an older couple strolling along the shore. I also saw a kid fishing much further out in a rowboat. But Frisky was on the shore, her ears at attention. She was barking at a man standing in the river. His U.S. Army fatigues were rolled up to his knees. His boots, olive drab shirt, and cap were piled at the edge of the river. He gracefully cast out a fishing net over the water. His close-cropped raven-black hair glistened in the sunlight.

I tiptoed toward the riverbank with the intention of grabbing Frisky and running. But I slipped on a muddy spot and fell. The soldier turned around. He smiled a friendly smile and laughed.

"You OK?" he asked. As he walked toward me, his bare feet getting coated with sand, I saw that his features were Asian. I had never met an Asian before. I felt my face turn red as he helped me up.

"Yeah, I'm okay," I said. I was more embarrassed than anything.

"What are you doing?" He spoke choppy English with an unfamiliar accent.

"Fishing," I muttered and brushed sand off my shorts.

"Me, too," he said, his dark eyes twinkling. "I love fishing. Back in my village,

Ong-noi and me fish every day on Song Tranh River."

I glanced at the ground. "I don't see your fishing pole."

"I use net. Big, big fish in river over there." He pointed to a dark green area of the river and held his hands three feet apart. "I come every weekend to catch big fish, but he get away."

"You need a fishing pole and bait," I said, relaxing a little. "Is it a yellow catfish?"

He crinkled his eyebrows into a question. "Cat-fish?"

With a stick I drew a fish in the sand, giving it long whiskers.

The soldier grinned. "That him. Big guy."

"My brother and father have been trying to catch Ol' Yeller for years. He must be thirty pounds. Keeps getting bigger and bigger. Show me where you saw him."

I picked up my fishing rod and followed the soldier out to a sandbar. The water gently sloshed around my ankles, then my knees, then touched the tips of my cutoffs before we crawled up onto the white island.

"There." He pointed to a greenish spot, then unfurled the net. It gracefully sailed through the air, plopped over the water and sank. He began drawing in the cord and hauling it back in. After he hoisted it on to the sandbar and emptied it, minnows, small perch, and crawdads leaped and squirmed. But no catfish. He tossed the catch back into the river, but not before I selected a lively minnow. I secured it on my hook, then cast out. The line whistled as it unreeled and the sinker smacked the water with a loud plop. I gently began reeling in.

"You good fisherman. Who teach you?" the guy asked me.

"Mostly my brother, Larry. He loved fishing more than anything in the world. He would have lived on the river, if he could."

The soldier nodded. "My village on river. Beautiful river."

"Who taught you to fish?"

"Ong-noi—my grandfather. He best fisherman in village. He skinny like a stick with white beard, but he strong. He say: 'To catch fish you must think like fish. When fish smell food, he get careless.'" The soldier heaved a sigh. "I want to be fisherman, too, like my grandfather and my father."

"I've never heard of fishing with a net," I said. "Where are you from?"

"Vietnam," he said proudly. "I am Trung Tran." He extended his hand. My heart jumped and a chill swept over my body.

"You're Vietnamese?" I said, recoiling from the hand. "What are you doing here? Shouldn't you be in the jungles fighting your stinking war?" My voice dripped ice, but I didn't care. I began reeling in the line as fast as I could.

✳

I saw the look of confusion cross his face as his smile faded. I knew I was being rude, but I had to get away.

"I go back soon," he said softly. "I come to America to train in helicopter. I become pilot so I can fight North Vietnamese."

His dark eyes sadly watched my jerky movements. With a set jaw I fought with the tangled fishing line. When Trung reached over to help free it, I pushed his hand away.

"I can do it myself," I hissed.

He watched in silence as I grew impatient and snapped the line in two with one vicious jerk. I heard him sigh.

"You no like Vietnamese," he stated calmly.

I didn't even want to look at his face again, but something inside me erupted before I could stop it.

"Vietnam ruined my family. If it weren't for you and your stupid war my brother would still be alive. He'd be right here fishing with me and you'd be back in your stupid village fishing with your stupid nets. I hate Vietnam! I hate it!"

He swallowed hard and his face clouded.

"I sorry for your brother. He very brave. All American brave. They come two years ago and help my village build wall to keep out the North Vietnamese. Americans play with kids. They laugh. I like Americans. My mother cook fish for soldier name Joe Bailey."

"When North Vietnamese discover that our village helped Americans, they come and kill our leaders. They kill my father and my old grandfather, my big brother and two cousin. They kill my mother for feeding fish to Joe Bailey. They burn our huts and take over our village, so I run away. I come to America to learn to fly chopper so I can help my country. I don't want America to fight our war, but I say thank you to all brave American who die."

I looked at his trembling chin and the water glistening on his dark irises. For a moment I didn't think he would be able to speak again, but he did.

"Sometime I say to myself, 'Why America send so many brave soldier to help little Vietnam? Must be that America love Vietnam like me.' Then I come to America and people look at me and say, 'Go home, we hate you! We hate stinky Vietnamese! What they mean—stinky?"

I saw the look of confusion, anger, and pain his face as he waited for my answer. I drew in a deep breath.

"It's not *you* they hate. It's the war." I paused. "I'm sorry about your family. I really am."

"I hate war too. But I love Vietnam. I always love Vietnam."

As Trung rolled up the fishing net we heard a loud splash. I saw the gray shape of a fish just beneath the green surface.

"Look! It's Ol' Yeller!" I whispered.

Trung reached into a little paper bag and tossed out a live cricket. The fish circled, then snapped, causing bubbles to dance on the surface. I knelt close to the water. The elusive monster fish was easily three feet long. How I wished I had not jerked my fishing line in two. I saw Trung unrolling his net.

"You'll never catch him with a net," I said.

"Who say?" Trung winked. He waited, like a cat over a goldfish bowl. Soon the fish disappeared.

"He's getting away!" I yelled. "Don't just stand there."

"I study his move. Think like fish." Trung tapped his forehead and tossed out another cricket.

A minute later the fish returned, gliding under the surface, snapping at the insect. Swift as a pouncing cat, Trung flung the net out a few feet away from the fish. As the net sank, he wiggled his hand in the water. The frightened catfish darted away from the hand toward the net. Trung waited, then jerked the cord with all his might. I grabbed one end of the net and together, grunting and struggling, we hauled the twisting, flapping fish onto the sandbar.

I stood up, my mouth open as I stared at the sleek gray body. It was scarred from years of fish hooks and close calls. The glassy eyes gleamed as it rolled on its back to reveal a yellow underbelly.

"Ol' Yeller. I don't believe it." I said. "I just don't believe it. What are you going to do with him?"

"He make plenty fish soup," Trung said, laughing. He stroked the soft underbelly and spoke to the fish as if it were a pet, carefully avoiding the poisonous whiskers and deadly sharp fins. I looked at the angry yellow eyes and the gills fighting desperately to breathe. A sinking feeling filled my heart and suddenly I wanted to cry again.

Trung looked up into my face and his grin faded.

"Ah, this fish too little for me," he said. With a grunt he shoved the fish back into the river. Ol' Yeller floated a second, then got his second wind and disappeared into the murky water.

"Why did you do that?" I asked.

Trung shrugged. "He not my fish. He your brother's fish. I have my own fish back in Song Tranh River. I go back and catch him someday." He glanced at the sun high above our heads.

"I go now. My friend need motorcycle for Big Date tonight." He sighed as he rolled up the net. "Someday when war over, maybe I have Big Date, too."

Trung slipped into his boots and shirt, then tugged his cap down low over his forehead.

"Goodbye, American girl," he said, extending his hand once again.

This time I shook it.

"Goodbye, Trung. Good luck."

I watched him climb onto an old motorcycle. He waved as it wheeled over the bank, spraying sand behind it.

I grabbed my fishing rod, woke Frisky from her snooze in the shade of a wild plum tree, and hurried back to the campsite. My parents sat on an old quilt, finishing up fried catfish and hushpuppies.

"Told you she'd be back in time for the peach ice cream," my father commented without missing a bite.

"So you did," my mother said. She rose and lifted the canister lid. Blobs of creamy white and yellow ice cream clung to the paddle.

"Want to lick the paddle?" she asked. "I remember how you and Larry used to—" She paused.

"—used to fight over the paddle?" I finished the sentence for her. I took the dripping utensil and tasted the sweet, creamy dessert. A million memories of Larry flooded my head and my heart.

"Yeah, I remember." I smiled and it felt good.

Breaking a Bad Habit

Many cultures have used stories with animal characters to help explain the sometimes odd habits and characteristics of humans. Sometimes the story shows how clever people can be and sometimes it shows us how silly we are. In this West African trickster tale, a rabbit and a monkey are going to show us that maybe we people have habits that are just too hard to break. No matter how hard we try.

ne day, in a West African forest, a rabbit and a monkey were sitting under a tree by a river. Every few minutes the monkey scratched himself with his long finger. First he scratched his neck. Then he scratched his ribs. Stretching his long arms around him, he even scratched his back. Scratching like this is a habit of monkeys.

The rabbit, close by, was no quieter. Every few minutes he sniffed the air. His nose wrinkled and twitched. His long ears flopped as he turned his head from one side to the other. This is the way of all rabbits. They seem always afraid that some danger is near.

Each animal noticed the movements of the other. And at last the rabbit could stand the monkey's scratching no longer.

"Why do you keep scratching yourself, Friend?" he said to the monkey who was then rubbing an ear. "You are not still a minute. Always, oh, all the time your nails are digging away at your hide. This is a most annoying habit you have."

Now nobody really enjoys being scolded. And so the monkey replied in the same annoyed tone of voice.

"My habit is no more annoying than yours, my good Rabbit. You do not keep still either. Your nose wrinkles and twitches. Your long ears keep flopping. Every few minutes you turn your silly head from one side to the other as if you were afraid."

"Well, perhaps I do twitch my nose and turn my head. But I can easily stop," the rabbit declared.

"I'll bet that you can't. Although I myself could easily keep from scratching, if I really wanted to." The monkey clasped both of his forepaws together.

They argued back and forth.

"I can stop my habit, but you cannot."

"If you can, I can." So it went until at last the monkey broke off.

"We'll make a test," he suggested. "We'll see which one of us is strong enough to break his bad habit. I'll bet you I can keep quite still for the whole afternoon. And I'll bet you cannot."

"Good!" There was nothing the rabbit could do but agree. "The one who moves first will lose the bet." He gave his head one last turn, and his nose one last twitch.

There they both sat, under the tree by the West African River. Not one move did either make. But each looked very unhappy.

Never in all his life did the skin of that monkey feel so dry and itchy. The rabbit's heart was cold with his fear of the unseen danger that might be behind him. But the monkey did not scratch. The rabbit did not turn his head.

It was not really very long. A beetle passing by had crawled only a few yards along the riverbank. But it seemed to the two animals that they had not moved for a whole day.

"What shall I do?" the poor rabbit was thinking hard. "I cannot keep still very much longer. If I could only sniff once! If I could but turn my head halfway round! Then it would not be so bad."

At the same time the monkey's hide was burning and itching.

"I cannot keep from scratching much longer," the beast said to himself. "If only I could rub myself without the rabbit seeing me."

It was the rabbit who spoke first.

"The time is long, Friend Monkey. Of course I am quite comfortable. I am entirely easy in my mind, Monkey. But the sun is still high in the sky. Why should we not tell each other a story to make the afternoon pass more quickly?"

"Well, why not?" The monkey suspected the rabbit was thinking of playing some trick. But he only added, "Yes, Rabbit, let us, each one, tell a story."

"I'll begin, Monkey. I will tell you of one day last month when I was far out of this forest. I was alone in a clearing, and there was not one bush to hide me."

Here the monkey broke in. He did not yet know what trick the rabbit had thought of, but he knew he should be prepared.

"Oh, Rabbit," he cried, "that very same thing once happened to me."

"Now don't interrupt." The rabbit was impatient to get on with his tale. "I heard a noise in the tall grass on this side of me." Like any storyteller he naturally turned his head to show how it was. "I saw some hyenas running toward me. One came from this side. One came from the other side." Again and again the rabbit's head was turned to illustrate his tale.

"Other hyenas came after them. From the right; from the left; from behind; and before me." Oh, now the rabbit was having a fine time, turning his head and twitching his nose. Anyone telling of so many dangers would have to do the same thing.

The monkey soon saw what his friend was up to. The moment the rabbit stopped to get breath, he began his own story.

"One day," he cried, "I went to the village on the other side of the forest. Some boys saw me there. And they began to throw stones at me.

"One stone hit me here." The monkey reached up and rubbed his neck to show where the stone hit. Oh, it did feel good to get in just that one little scratch.

"Another stone hit me here." The monkey rubbed his shoulder. "Another! Another! And another stone came." Now the creature's paw was flying from one itching place to another.

The rabbit burst into a laugh. He laughed and he laughed. The monkey laughed too. Each guessed the other's reason for telling his story that way.

The two animals laughed so hard that they had to hold onto each other to keep from rolling into the river.

"Well! Well!" the monkey cried. "I have not yet lost the bet."

"No more than I," said the rabbit. "We were each of us only telling a tale as it should be told."

"But we must agree, Friend," he continued, "it's very hard indeed to break a bad habit. No one ever easily changes his ways. Let us worry no more."

So the rabbit's nose wrinkled and twitched again as often as he wished. His long ears flopped as his round head turned every few minutes from one side to the other.

The monkey's paws scratched his hide wherever it itched. And from that day to this no member of either of these animal families has kept still very long unless he was asleep.

You may wish to engage students in a discussion about habits—good ones and bad ones. How do we start good ones? How do we break bad ones?

Bacteria: The Good, the Bad, and the Stinky

by Joy Masoff

You can't see 'em; you can't hear 'em; you can't taste 'em. But, oh boy, can they make you smelly or sick! In this science article you're about to hear, you'll learn the nasty truth . . . about bacteria.

Bacteria are tiny living things (known as microorganisms) that cover the entire earth. They live in the dirt and deep in the sea. They float through the air and thrive in the bodies of every living thing. They are *not* plants, *not* animals, *not* fungi. Instead they belong to a group of living things called MONERA (*moan-air-ah*).

Most bacteria are so small that if you put 10,000 of them in a row, they would measure only about an inch. (And getting your hands on 10,000 bacteria is a snap. One bacterium can divide into a million bacteria in half a day!) Of course, there always has to be an exception to every rule. A monster bacteria has just been discovered lurking in the reeking, sulfurous muck of the ocean bottom near the coast of Namibia in Africa. These are big guys, big enough that you can see them without using a microscope. Each is about the size of the period at the end of this sentence. That may not seem huge, but in the bacteria world, that's a King Kong of a germ.

What do bacteria love to do most of all? Munch! They munch on the oil in our skin and the partially digested dinner in our guts. They'll invade the flesh of a dead cow and the grease in your kitchen drain. They'll even take on a half-mile-wide oil spill!

Most bacteria are totally cool little microbes (another name for microorganisms). Some turn raw sewage into chemicals that help plants grow. Then there are the ones that specialize in devouring grease, eating pond scum, or lapping up those huge oil spills. Good bacteria such as these are actually sold by laboratories around the world. Other good bacteria help break down animal hides so they can be turned into shoes, handbags, briefcases, and those cool motorcycle jackets. Other ones are used to make vaccines, medicines, yogurt, and even tea!

Then there are the "geeky" bacteria, like the ones that create a stink in our armpits. They're not exactly harmful, but they sure are annoying.

Finally, there are the "bully" bacteria that can make us sick by causing food poisoning, strep throat, pneumonia, diarrhea, and other big-time problems. They come in different shapes, just like the bullies at school. There are tall, skinny ones, round, pudgy ones, spiral ones, and curvy ones. And just like the school bullies, they can make your life miserable.

One of the main ways that bully bacteria are spread is through bad hygiene. Translation? Not washing your hands after you go to the bathroom. Remember that half of what your body's getting rid of when you poop is bacteria. Some of it is harmless, but some is not. As you wipe, bacteria can leap onto your hands. Once on your hands, the bacteria start to reproduce like crazy. If a person who works at the local burger joint doesn't wash, those bacteria creep into everything he handles—the burgers and fries and milk shakes. And before you can say "I think I'm gonna hurl," you—and everyone else who had the bad luck to eat there that day—will be tossing cookies!

Other times, sickness starts when bacteria that live aboard one animal make the move to another. A perfectly healthy chicken's guts are crawling with salmonella bacteria that help the chicken digest all that chicken feed. But when that same bacteria gets into our intestines, disaster can strike. "But," you say, "it's not like I'm kissing a chicken." True, but chances are you're eating one! Under-cooked chicken can give you salmonella. Even eating the uncooked egg that has been beaten into brownie batter can make you pretty sick, so don't lick that spoon!

Some nonliving things, such as air conditioners, can hide bacteria cities. Certain types of these microbes adore the warm wetness that's created by air conditioner motors. And the air blowing from them propels millions of bacteria into the air— *and* the lungs of whoever happens to be in the room! Before you know what's hit you, you'll be shaking with chills and flushed with a fever from Legionnaires' disease.

Fortunately, other living creatures, namely fungi, can beat the bully bacteria up. That's basically what that nasty pink stuff is that your doctor gives you for ear infections or strep throat—a mess of bigger, meaner critters. Kind of like the principal and the dean of students on the warpath. These ANTIBIOTICS (that's what the pink stuff is called) destroy bacteria. And, boy, are we grateful to them. Their only downside: They wipe out the good bacteria (those that break down food) along with the bad. That's why lots of us end up with the trots when we take antibiotics. But fear not! The good-guy bacteria will be back! And you can even help bring them back faster by eating yogurt that contains active acidophilus cultures.

All living things rot . . . sometimes quickly, sometimes very, v-e-r-y slowly. Rotting is, believe it or not, a part of growing—of living. Without rotting, the corpses of everything that has died since life on earth began would be piled up all over the place! Bacteria help make that rotting happen. Let's say that a caterpillar gets squooshed on the street. A goner, right? No heartbeat. No breathing. But the bacteria living on the caterpillar are still chugging along. They invade the tissue and alter the chemical makeup of that caterpillar, breaking it down into smaller and smaller bits until it disappears and is reabsorbed into the earth.

So let's have a round of applause for those hard-working bacteria. If it weren't for them, you'd be stepping on a mile-high mound of dead bodies on your way to school every day!

New Kid

by Patricia Hermes

Imagine that it's the beginning of the school year and you are a new kid in school. What do you think are going to be some of the hardest things about being the new kid?

Now imagine that you are a new kid in school—but it's the middle of the year. What's probably going to be difficult about that?

Listen to how Emma deals with being the new kid.

y sister, Meggie, wasn't scared.

Sam, her twin, wasn't scared.

I wasn't scared.

Well, I was only a little scared.

It was the first day going to our new school, and in the car next to me, Meggie was jumping up and down on the seat, even with her seat belt on.

"I can see the school!" she yelled. "Look! We're almost there!"

"Hey, yeah!" Sam yelled. "School. We're almost there. I can see it."

Mom laughed. "Yes, Meggie and Sam," she said. "I can see it too."

"Don't yell in my ear!" I said to the twins.

Mom pulled the car up and parked at the sign that said Parents Drop Off. She turned and looked at me over the seat.

"Are you all right, Emma?" she said.

"I'm fine!" I said.

"A little scared?" Mom said.

I shrugged. "No."

Actually, yes.

"I'm not scared," Sam said.

I just rolled my eyes at him. It was easy for him and Meggie. They're just in kindergarten. I'm in fifth. And going to a new school is different when you're older, especially like now, starting in the middle of the school year. Still, I had rehearsed just how to act. I would do what I did in my old school, what I did in my ballet classes, what I did when I first started horseback riding lessons. I would act really, really friendly. I would smile and talk to people. And even if I felt a little shy, I wouldn't let it show.

I'm pretty good at it. Actually, I'm very good at it. Mom is a clothing designer and is very good at meeting new people. She taught me to always act friendly, even if I feel shy inside. This morning, though, I was even more nervous than I'd thought I'd be. Because all I could think of was my old school. And Dorothy.

But I told myself I wasn't Dorothy. I wasn't at all like Dorothy.

"Want me to walk you to your class before I take Meggie and Sam?" Mom said.

"NO!" I said. I glared at her. We had

been here last Friday to meet the teacher, Mrs. Kaye. There was no need to have Mom walk me like a baby. Besides, if kids see your mom bringing you in, they stare.

"OK, Emma," Mom said. She leaned over the seat and gave me a kiss on the forehead. "Remember. Heads up! You'll have a new best friend before the day is over!"

I nodded, jumped out of the car, ran into school, and then went down the fifth-grade hall. I found my room, and in the hall outside, my coat hook with my name over it. And I did just what I had been practicing. When someone looked at me, I smiled—not a big fake goofy smile, just a plain friendly smile. And I waited for people to smile back.

In the hall, lots of people were crowding around, hanging up coats on coat hooks, putting books and boots and stuff underneath. A couple of girls did smile back. One, a girl who was wearing black velvet tights with her hair in a ponytail, she looked like she wanted to speak to me, but then she didn't. And another girl, with long blond hair, and little gold hoop earrings, she started to say something, but the ponytail girl pulled her into the classroom. Another girl, who was shorter than everyone else, with big dark eyes, she actually spoke to me.

"Hi," she said. But then she ducked her head like she was shy, and hurried into the classroom.

After they were gone, I looked at their names over their coat hooks. Amanda was the ponytail one. Maybe she'd be my friend, just like the other Amanda in my old school. The one with the earrings was Gisella. And the one

who said hi, and then ducked her head, that was Rebecca.

I hung up my coat, then picked up my books. I thought of what Mom had said: You'll make a best friend before the day is over.

But what if I didn't? What if I never made a new friend in this school? What if I ended up like Dorothy?

I went into the classroom.

Mrs. Kaye was sitting at her desk, and when she saw me, she got up and came to me. "Emma!" she said, putting an arm around my shoulder. "Welcome!"

Right away, everyone in the class looked at me.

I looked back at them, trying to look friendly, even though my heart was thumping kind of hard. I thought of Dorothy, how shy and scared she'd seemed, how she wouldn't even look at people that first day she'd come to my old school. I wondered if she had felt like I did now.

Mrs. Kaye looked around the classroom. "Amanda!" she said, "You remember meeting Emma last week? Will you be Emma's helper today?"

Amanda shook her head. "I can't," she said. "I have orchestra this morning."

"Oh, that's right," Mrs. Kaye said. "Gisella? Why don't you show Emma around today."

Gisella looked at Amanda. Amanda shrugged and rolled her eyes.

Gisella turned back to Mrs. Kaye. "I have early dismissal for an orthodontist appointment."

"Well, that's not until later this afternoon," Mrs. Kaye said. She turned to me. We'll put your desk next to Gisella's. She can show you the routine." She looked up. "All right, Gisella?"

Gisella nodded, but she didn't look too happy. I also noticed that she and Amanda were giving each other looks. Then they both looked at me, and the two of them giggled.

I tried to think why they would laugh. They don't even know me! Was I dressed funny? I looked around the room. I was wearing overalls. But other girls were wearing overalls too, including Rebecca, who had said hello to me.

Did I have food on my mouth? A juice mustache from breakfast? Toast crumbs glued to my chin? I tried to wipe my mouth without being too obvious about it.

I sat down next to Gisella.

"What do we have first?" I asked.

"You'll just have to watch," Gisella said. "We have projects due today."

"What kind of projects?" I said.

But she didn't answer. She and Amanda put their heads together and began whispering.

The whole day went on like that. Nobody was actually mean to me. But nobody tried to be friendly, either.

I kept thinking of Dorothy. She had come in new in the middle of last year, just like me. But she was kind of strange. She dressed in funny looking clothes—everybody called her "rag coat," and she wore black rubber boots every day, even when it wasn't raining. When we went on class trips, the only person who would be her partner was the teacher. People said she didn't care about making friends. But one day I found her in the gym locker room, all by herself, crying. And I felt so bad. I wanted to say something to make her feel better. But I told myself she wouldn't

want me to. So I just pretended I didn't see her and walked away.

What if this whole year was like that? What if they all treated me like we treated Dorothy?

When Mom picked me up that day, I just told her everything went fine. But as soon as I got home, I went right to my room. I wrote a letter to my best friend Amanda.

"I hate it here," I wrote. "I miss you, I miss you, I miss you. Meggie and Sam think it's great. The girls in my class are mean. I felt like I was INVISIBLE. It's going to be a horrible year. It must be lonely for you there without me.

"Remember Dorothy last year?"

"Love from Emma."

At school next day, things weren't much better. At lunch recess, I tried hard to be friendly, but nobody was friendly back. It was like everybody already had a best friend. I even went to where the girls were bunched up around the swing set, but they all stopped talking when I got there. Once, one of the boys, Carl, pushed me. I wanted to run away. But then I decided to push him back.

He didn't do it again.

After a while, I got permission from the recess monitor to go inside to the bathroom, just to get away. Rebecca was just coming out as I went in. "Hi," she said. This time, she didn't duck her head.

"Hi," I said back.

"You've got something on your coat," she said. "Turn around."

I turned my back to her. "What is it?" I said.

"Just a dumb sticker," she said.

I could feel her pulling at my jacket.

But then she said, "It won't come off. Your mom will have to wash it."

I took off my jeans jacket, turned it around and looked at it. It was one of those gross stickers you get in the gumball machine. It had a picture of an alien creature on it, with a green face with worms gushing out of its mouth. It had writing on the bottom: *Go Back To Your Planet.*

I felt tears come up to my eyes, and I blinked hard, blinking them back.

"I bet it was one of the boys," Rebecca said, "Carl, probably. Don't let him bother you. Sometimes he's weird."

That was nice of her to say. But I felt like the weird one.

"Where do you live?" she asked.

"On Peppertree," I said.

"I live right behind Peppertree," Rebecca said. "Do you take the bus?"

I shook my head. "I'll be walking soon. But my mom is driving for now."

"I walk too," Rebecca said.

The bell rang, and we started off to our room. As we went, I was able to peel off the sticker, but it left some gummy stuff on my jacket.

"Don't worry about the sticker," Rebecca said as we went into the classroom.

But I did worry. A lot. And suddenly, in my head, I had this picture of Dorothy and her raggy coat, and all of us laughing. I had another picture of Dorothy standing near me with her lunch tray, hoping I'd make room for her at my table—and I'd pretended not to notice.

I worried even more when I came into the classroom, and saw Gisella and Amanda whispering, looking at me and giggling.

Suddenly, I couldn't help it. I walked right up to them.

"Did you want to tell me something?" I said, sweetly.

Gisella blushed.

"Uh, no, uh, we were just talking about soccer," Amanda said.

"Really?" I said. I knew it was a big lie.

I went to my seat, but I kept looking at them. Why would they act that way? Why would they whisper about me and stick gross stickers on me just because . . .

Because I was new. Because they didn't know who I really was. Because they didn't know any better.

They didn't know better. And I hadn't known better, either.

With Dorothy.

When I got home that day, I went right into my room again. I told Mom I had a lot of homework, which I did. But I had some other work to do, too—some leftover work.

I sat on the floor, and leaned back against my bed, using my knees for a desk, and I started to write a letter. I wrote the whole thing without really even thinking about it. I wrote about how lonely it felt being new. I wrote about a whole lot of stuff. And then, before I could change my mind, I put it in an envelope, put a name on it, and sealed it tight. I knew Mom still had a phone book from our old town.

I was just finishing when I heard Mom calling me. "Emma! Telephone. For you."

I ran down the stairs. For me? Who could it be calling me? Was it long distance? Was it Amanda?

No. It was Rebecca. Rebecca from school! "Want to walk to school together tomorrow?" she asked.

"OK, Rebecca," I said. And we agreed to meet at the corner in the morning.

After I hung up, Mom said, "I told you you'd make a friend in no time."

I smiled, but I didn't answer.

"Know why?" Mom said. "Because you're friendly and kind. You know how to be a friend."

I didn't answer. Mom was only half right. I was friendly. But I hadn't always been so kind. Not to everyone. I knew a little more about that now. And I couldn't wait to mail that letter to Dorothy.

The Tell-Tale Heart
A Retelling of the Short Story
by Edgar Allan Poe

Mention the name Edgar Allan Poe and some people will shudder. Why? Because Edgar Allan Poe's stories have been thrilling—and chilling—readers and listeners for years. See how this one, which is based on the original, makes you feel.

I can't say how the idea first entered my brain, but once it was there, it haunted me day and night. There wasn't any reason for it. I liked the old man. He never did anything to hurt me, and I wasn't after his money.

I think it was his eyes! Yes, that was it! One of his eyes looked like the eye of a vulture —pale gray with a film over it. Whenever it looked at me, my blood ran cold. I made up my mind to kill the old man and get rid of that eye forever.

I made my move slowly. Every night at midnight, I opened his door very gently, poked my head in, and shined a lantern on his vulture eye.

I did this for seven nights—every night just at midnight. But his eye was always closed, so I could not bring myself to do what I had to do. It was not the old man who bothered me. It was his evil eye.

On the eighth night, I was even more careful than usual. I thought about the fact that I was opening the door and that he wasn't even dreaming of my secret thought. I had to laugh.

Perhaps he heard me. He moved suddenly. His room was dark, so I knew he couldn't see the door opening.

I had my head in and was about to turn the lantern on, but my thumb slipped on the tin switch. The old man sat up in bed, crying, "Who's there?"

I kept still, not moving an inch. Finally, I heard a slight groan, and I knew it was a groan of terror—terror in the face of death.

I knew the terror the old man felt and I felt sorry for him, although I laughed inside. I knew he had been lying awake ever since the first slight noise. His fears had grown ever since. He tried to tell himself, "It is nothing but the wind in the chimney . . . It is only a mouse crossing the floor . . . It is just a cricket.

I waited a long time, and I turned the lantern up a little bit. I was careful. Only a single ray shot out and fell on his vulture eye.

The eye was wide open! I grew angry as I looked at it. I could see it perfectly— that dull gray eye with an ugly film over it chilled my bones.

Then I heard it, a low, dull, quick

sound. It was like the sound a watch makes when it's wrapped in cotton. It was the beating of the old man's heart. It made my anger grow, but even then I kept still. I hardly breathed at all. I kept the ray of light shining on his eye. The beating of his heart grew quicker and quicker, and louder and louder.

In the dead hour of the night, in the awful silence of that old house, that noise terrified me. Yet for a few minutes longer, I stood still.

The beating grew louder, louder! Then a new fear grabbed me. The sound was so loud that a neighbor might hear it!

With a loud yell, I turned the lantern up and leaped into the room. He screamed once, only once, before I dragged him to the floor and lay the heavy mattress over him.

I smiled. The deed was almost done. For many minutes his heart beat on with a muffled sound.

This didn't bother me. The sound would not be heard through the wall.

Finally it stopped, and the old man was dead. I removed the bed and looked at the body. I put my hand on his heart and held it there many minutes—no heartbeat. His eye would not trouble me ever again.

I worked quickly but silently as I pulled up three boards from the floor. Then I slipped the old man's body into the space below and replaced the boards so well that no human eye could have found anything wrong. Ha! Ha!

Soon after I'd finished, someone knocked at the door. It was three policemen who said that a neighbor had heard a scream. I smiled and invited them in. The scream, I said, was my own.

I'd had a nightmare. I told them the old man was away in the country. I told them to search the house—search it well.

Finally, I took them into his room and asked them to sit down. I placed my chair on the floorboards above his body.

The policemen were satisfied since I seemed very much at ease. But then I felt myself getting pale. My head hurt and I imagined a pounding in my ears, but the policemen just sat there, talking and talking. The pounding in my ears grew louder. Finally, I decided that the terrible noise was not just in my head.

I tried talking more quickly and in a louder voice, but the sound got louder too. What could I do? It was a low, dull, quick sound. It was like the sound a watch makes when it is wrapped in cotton.

The police didn't seem to hear it, so I kept talking, even more quickly. The noise got louder.

The men kept talking. Was it possible that they did not hear it? No, they heard, and they knew! They were making fun of my terror.

Anything was better than this. I couldn't stand their smiles any longer. I had to scream—or I'd die. The noise got louder, louder, louder!

"Enough!" I screamed. "I admit it! Tear up the floor! Here, here! It is the beating of his hideous heart."

My Rows and Piles of Coins

by Tololwa M. Mollel

The author of the story you are about to hear is from the African country called Tanzania. In this story, you'll meet Saruni, a young Tanzanian boy who every week counts the coins in his box, dreaming about the day he will buy himself his very own bicycle.

READER'S TIP

* There are some words in this story that may be unfamiliar to listeners. They are:
  Yeyo [yeh YOH]: mother
  Chapati [chah PAH tee]: fried flat bread
  Sambusa [sahm BOO sah]: dough stuffed with spiced vegetables, meat, or both
  Murete [MOO reh ta]: a term of affection for an older family member

After a good day at the market, my mother, Yeyo, gave me five whole ten-cent coins. I gaped at the money until Yeyo nudged me. "Saruni, what are you waiting for? Go and buy yourself something."

I plunged into the market. I saw roasted peanuts, chapati, rice cakes, and sambusa. There were wooden toy trucks, kites, slingshots, and marbles. My heart beat excitedly. I wanted to buy everything, but I clutched my coins tightly in my pocket.

At the edge of the market, I stopped. In a neat sparkling row stood several big new bicycles. One of them was decorated all over with red and blue.

That's what I would buy!

For some time now, Murete, my father, had been teaching me to ride his big, heavy bicycle. If only I had a bicycle of my own!

A gruff voice startled me.

"What are you looking for, little boy?"

I turned and bumped into a tall skinny man, who laughed at my confusion. Embarrassed, I hurried back to Yeyo.

That night, I dropped five ten-cent coins into my secret money box. It held other ten-cent coins Yeyo had given me for helping with market work on Saturdays. By the dim light of a lantern, I feasted my eyes on the money. I couldn't believe it was all mine.

I emptied the box,
arranged all the coins in piles
and the piles in rows.
Then I counted the coins
and thought about the bicycle
I longed to buy.

Every day after school, when I wasn't helping Yeyo to prepare supper, I asked Murete if I could ride his bicycle. He held the bicycle steady while I rode around, my toes barely touching the pedals.

Whenever Murete let go, I wobbled, fell off, or crashed into things and among coffee trees. Other children from the neighborhood had a good laugh watching me.

Go on, laugh, I thought, sore but determined. Soon I would be like a cheetah on wheels, racing on errands with my very own bicycle!

Saturday after Saturday, we took goods to market, piled high on Yeyo's head and on my squeaky old wooden wheelbarrow. We sold dried beans and maize, pumpkins, spinach, bananas, firewood, and eggs.

My money box grew heavier.
I emptied the box,
arranged the coins in piles
and the piles in rows.
Then I counted the coins
and thought about
the blue and red bicycle.

After several more lessons Murete let me ride on my own while he shouted instructions. *"Eyes up, arms straight, keep pedaling, slow down!"* I enjoyed the breeze on my face, the pedals turning smoothly under my feet, and, most of all, Yeyo's proud smile as she watched me ride. How surprised she would be to see my new bicycle! And how grateful she would be when I used it to help her on market days!

The heavy March rains came. The ground became so muddy, nobody went to market. Instead, I helped Yeyo with house chores. When it wasn't raining, I helped Murete on the coffee farm. We pruned the coffee trees and put fallen leaves and twigs around the coffee stems. Whenever I could, I practiced riding Murete's bicycle.

It stopped raining in June. Not long after, school closed. Our harvest—fresh maize and peas, sweet potatoes, vegetables, and fruits—was so big, we went to market on Saturdays *and* Wednesdays. My money box grew heavier and heavier.

I emptied the box,
arranged the coins in piles
and the piles in rows.
Then I counted the coins
and thought about the bicycle
I would buy.

A few days later I grew confident enough to try to ride a loaded bicycle. With Murete's help, I strapped a giant pumpkin on the carrier behind me. When I attempted to pedal, the bicycle wobbled so dangerously that Murete, alongside me, had to grab it.

"All right, Saruni, the load is too heavy for you," he said, and I got off. Mounting the bicycle to ride back to the house, he sighed wearily. "And hard on my bones, which are getting too old for pedaling."

I practiced daily with smaller loads, and slowly I learned to ride a loaded bicycle. No more pushing the squeaky old wheelbarrow, I thought. I would ride with my load tall and proud on my bicycle— just like Murete!

On the first Saturday after school opened in July, we went to market as usual. Late in the afternoon, after selling all we had, Yeyo sat talking with another trader.

I set off into the crowd. I wore an old coat Murete had handed down to me for chilly July days like today. My precious coins were wrapped in various bundles inside the oversize pockets of the coat.

I must be the richest boy in the world, I thought, feeling like a king. *I can buy anything.*

The tall skinny man was polishing his bicycles as I came up. "I want to buy a bicycle," I said, and brought out my bundles of coins.

The man whistled in wonder as I unwrapped the money carefully on his table. "How many coins have you got there?"

Proudly, I told him. "Three hundred and five."

"Three hundred and . . . five," he muttered. "Mmh, that's . . . thirty shillings and fifty cents." He exploded with laughter. "A whole bicycle . . . for thirty shillings . . . and fifty cents?"

His laugh followed me as I walked away with my bundles of coins, deeply disappointed.

On our way home, Yeyo asked what was wrong.

I had to tell her everything.

"You saved all your money for a bicycle to help me?" she asked. I could tell she was amazed and touched. "How nice of you!" As for the tall skinny man, she scoffed, "Oi! What does he know? Of course you will buy a bicycle. One day you will."

Her kind words did not cheer me.

The next afternoon, the sound of a pikipiki filled the air, *tuk-tuk-tuk-tuk-tuk*. I came out of the house and stared in astonishment. Murete was perched on an orange motorbike.

He cut the engine and dismounted. Then, chuckling at my excited questions about the pikipiki, he headed into the house.

When Murete came out, Yeyo was with him, and he was wheeling his bicycle. "I want to sell this to you. For thirty shillings and fifty cents." He winked at me.

Surprised, I stared at Murete. How did he know about my secret money box? I hadn't told him anything.

Then, suddenly, I realized the wonderful thing that had just happened. "My bicycle, I have my very own bicycle!" I said, and it didn't matter at all that it wasn't decorated with red and blue. Within moments, I had brought Murete my money box.

Murete gave Yeyo the box. Yeyo, in turn, gave it to me. Puzzled, I looked from Yeyo to Murete and to Yeyo again. "You're giving it . . . back to me?"

Yeyo smiled. "It's a reward for all your help to us."

"Thank you, thank you!" I cried gleefully.

The next Saturday, my load sat tall and proud on my bicycle, which I walked importantly to market. I wasn't riding it because Yeyo could never have kept up.

Looking over at Yeyo, I wished she didn't have to carry such a big load on her head.

If only I had a cart to pull behind my bicycle, I thought, *I could lighten her load!*

That night I emptied the box,
arranged all the coins in piles
and the piles in rows.
Then I counted the coins
and thought about the cart
I would buy . . . .

I Never Said I Wasn't Difficult

by Sara Holbrook

As you listen to this poem, ask yourself, "Is it possible for one person to think and feel all these things?" See if you can relate to what she is saying.

I never said I wasn't difficult,
I mostly want my way.
Sometimes I talk back or pout
and don't have much to say.

I've been known to yell, "So what,"
when I'm stepping out of bounds.
I want you there for me and yet,
I don't want you around.

I wish I had more privacy
and never had to be alone.
I want to run away.
I'm scared to leave my home.
I'm too tired to be responsible.
I wish that I were boss.
I want to blaze new trails.
I'm terrified that I'll get lost.

I wish an answer came
every time I asked you, "why?"
I wish you weren't a know-it-all.
Why do you question when I'm bored?
I won't be cross-examined.
I hate to be ignored.

I know,
I shuffle messages like cards,
some to show and some to hide.
But, if you think I'm hard to live with
you should try me on inside.

READER'S TIP

* Because this poem is a list of contradictions, it can be very effective to pause briefly between statements.

"I Have a Dream"

by Dr. Martin Luther King, Jr.

When Dr. Martin Luther King, Jr., gave this famous speech at the Lincoln Memorial in Washington, D.C., on August 28, 1963, the United States was ripe for change. African Americans had been free of slavery's chains for nearly 100 years. But in the South, unfair laws still kept them from real freedom. African Americans could not drink from the same water fountains as whites, eat at the same restaurants, or attend the same schools.

Members of the Civil Rights Movement were actively fighting these laws. Dr. King, one of the leaders of the movement, arranged boycotts, led protest marches, and served as a spokesperson. This speech was a powerful reminder that the U.S. still fell short of the promises it guaranteed in the Constitution.

Five score years ago, a great American, in whose symbolic shadow we stand, signed the Emancipation Proclamation. This momentous decree came as a great beacon light of hope to millions of Negro slaves who had been seared in the flames of withering injustice . . .

But one hundred years later, we must face the tragic fact that the Negro is still not free.

One hundred years later, the life of the Negro is still sadly crippled by the manacles of segregation and the chains of discrimination . . .

. . . In a sense we have come to our nation's capital to cash a check. When the architects of our republic wrote the magnificent words of the Constitution and the Declaration of Independence, they were signing a promissory note to which every American was to [inherit].

This note was a promise that all men would be guaranteed the inalienable rights of life, liberty, and the pursuit of happiness. It is obvious today that America has defaulted on this promissory note insofar as her citizens of color are concerned. Instead of honoring this sacred obligation, America has given the Negro people a bad check . . . We refuse to believe that the bank of justice is bankrupt . . .

READER'S TIP

Students will better understand the beginning of this speech if they know these terms:

* promissory note
* bankrupt

. . . So we have come to cash this check—a check that will give us upon demand the riches of freedom and the security of justice . . .

. . .It would be fatal for the nation to overlook the urgency of the moment and to underestimate the determination of the Negro . . .

. . .Those who hope that the Negro needed to blow off steam and will now be content will have a rude awakening if the nation returns to business as usual. There will be neither rest nor tranquility in America until the Negro is granted his citizenship rights... But there is something that I must say to my people who stand on the warm threshold which leads into the palace of justice. In the process of gaining our rightful place we must not be guilty of wrongful deeds. Let us not seek to satisfy our thirst for freedom by drinking from the cup of bitterness and hatred . . .

We cannot walk alone. And as we walk, we must make the pledge that we shall march ahead. We cannot turn back. There are those who [ask], "When will you be satisfied?" We can never be satisfied as long as our bodies, heavy with the fatigue of travel, cannot gain lodging in the motels of the highways and the hotels of the cities. We cannot be satisfied as long as the Negro's basic mobility is from a smaller ghetto to a larger one. We can never be satisfied as long as a Negro in Mississippi cannot vote and a Negro in New York believes he has nothing for which to vote. No, no, we are not satisfied, and we will not be satisfied until justice rolls down like waters and righteousness like a mighty stream.

I am not unmindful that some of you have come here out of great trials and tribulations. . . . Some of you have come from areas where your quest for freedom left you battered by the storms of persecution and staggered by the winds of police brutality . . .

Go back to Mississippi, go back to Alabama, go back to Georgia, go back to Louisiana, go back to the slums and ghettos of our northern cities, knowing that somehow this situation can and will be changed . . .

I say to you today, my friends, that in spite of the difficulties and frustrations of the moment, I still have a dream. It is a dream deeply rooted in the American dream.

I have a dream that one day this nation will rise up and live out the true meaning of its creed: "We hold these truths to be self-evident: that all men are created equal."

I have a dream that one day on the red hills of Georgia the sons of former slaves and the sons of former slaveowners will be able to sit down together at a table of brotherhood.

I have a dream that one day even the state of Mississippi, a desert state, sweltering with the heat of injustice and oppression, will be transformed into an oasis of freedom and justice.

I have a dream that my four little children will one day live in a nation where they will not be judged by the color of their skin but by the content of their character.

I have a dream today.

I have a dream that one day down in Alabama . . . little black boys and black girls will be able to join hands with little white boys and white girls and walk together as sisters and brothers.

I have a dream today.

This will be the day when all of God's children will be able to sing with a new meaning, "My country, 'tis of thee, sweet land of liberty, of thee I sing. Land where my fathers died, land of the pilgrim's pride, from every mountainside, let freedom ring."

And if America is to be a great nation, this must become true. So let freedom ring from the prodigious hilltops of New Hampshire. Let freedom ring from the mighty mountains of New York. Let freedom ring from the heightening Alleghenies of Pennsylvania! Let freedom ring from the snowcapped Rockies of Colorado! Let freedom ring from the curvaceous peaks of California! But not only that; let freedom ring from Stone Mountain of Georgia! Let freedom ring from Lookout Mountain of Tennessee! Let freedom ring from every hill and every molehill of Mississippi. From every mountainside, let freedom ring.

When we let freedom ring, when we let it ring from every village and every hamlet, from every state and every city, we will be able to speed up that day when all of God's children, black men and white men, Jews and Gentiles, Protestants and Catholics, will be able to join hands and sing in the words of the old Negro spiritual, "Free at last! Free at last! Thank God Almighty, we are free at last!"

READER'S TIP

* Much of the power of Dr. King's speech came not just from his choice of words, but also from the slow, steady, and rhythmic pace in which he read them.

  As you read aloud, pause frequently so that listeners can feel the power and impact of his words.

* Here are the definitions to some of the key words in Dr. King's speech:

  Prodigious: enormous

  Hamlet: small village

Just a Pigeon

by Dennis Brindell Bradin

Everyone knows what a pigeon is—it's a bird. But pigeon is also a word used for someone who is easily fooled. You're about to hear a story where maybe—just maybe—both definitions of the word pigeon are used. You decide.

For Terrence, life seemed a little rough at times—going to high school, pumping gas after school and Saturdays, and studying late into the night. He often had to tell himself, "You've got to keep at it to go to college."

But now, a Friday, Terrence McCray felt good. He was walking home after work with a paycheck in his pocket.

He was thinking about his date the next night with Deborah, when he saw the injured pigeon. It was in the gutter. Several people were hurrying by.

It's just a pigeon. It's just a pigeon with a busted wing, he told himself. Some people walk by *people*. So why should I do anything for a pigeon? But it looked so helpless and scared.

He didn't want to pick it up, because he knew that pigeons sometimes carry diseases. So he went inside a grocery store and got a paper bag. When he came back outside, he hoped the pigeon would be gone. But it was still there.

"Come on, pigeon," he said, bending over with the bag. He felt like a fool. Some people had stopped to stare. But he picked up a twig and gently pushed the bird into the bag and carried it to his house.

Terrence's mother hadn't gotten angry when she saw the bird. She hardly ever got angry at him. She just said, "You're good-hearted, Terrence. But you can't take the burden of the world on your shoulders. You can try to help that bird. But . . . get it out of my kitchen."

After dinner, his mother got ready for work. Terrence rushed out and bought some birdseed.

When he got back, his mother was in her nurse's uniform. She said, "You brought the bird here. So you decide what to do with it."

Terrence fed the pigeon. Then he put the bird in the shoebox out on the porch.

Later, he could hear the bird cooing sadly. "Maybe I should have left it in the street," he said to himself. "It will probably die, anyway."

On Monday, between classes, Terrence looked up "Veterinarians" in the phone book. He got out his cell phone, and dialed a number.

"Pigeon?" the doctor said. "Broken wing? I could try to fix it."

"How much will it cost?" Terrence asked.

"I couldn't tell. It could be expensive.

If I can fix the wing, the bird will have to stay here a while. But you would have to pay me all at once."

After history class, Willie Barnes asked Terrence to shoot baskets in the gym.

"I can't, Willie," he said. "See, I found this pigeon with a busted wing. I've got to take it to the vet before work."

"What?" Willie said. "Spending money on a pigeon?"

Thad Lanier had stopped to listen. He stared at Terrence and said, "So many people in this world need help. And you spend money on a pigeon?"

"I saw it in a gutter," Terrence tried to explain. "I couldn't help it."

But Thad had turned and walked off with Willie, shaking his head.

Terrence took the pigeon to the vet. Dr. Landis said, "I've got to admit, this is my first pigeon. But I think I can fix its wing. Leave it here and give me a call tomorrow."

The next day, Terrence called Dr. Landis. He learned that the bird's wing had been set, and it was doing well.

Terrence was glad about the bird. But he was worried about the money. Besides that, Thad kept making remarks. One afternoon, just before history class started, Thad went too far.

"Talk about your future leaders!" Thad said. "How about Terrence here? He's spending his money on a pigeon."

"A what?" Deborah asked. "Is that why we couldn't go to the movies, Terrence?"

"Yeah," Thad said. "He found a sick pigeon, and he's paying for it to get well. Meanwhile, poor people don't have enough to eat." Excited by his own voice, Thad added, "Hey, who's the *real* pigeon?"

Terrence got out of his seat and rushed at Thad. Just then, the teacher walked in.

Terrence didn't care. He raised his fist. But as he saw Thad's frightened face, he all of a sudden felt sorry for him. He also knew why he had saved the pigeon.

"It was in trouble," he said. "It was alive, like us. If you walk past an animal one day, who knows—the next thing you might walk past is a person."

"What's all this?" the teacher asked as she came back into the room. "Nothing," Terence said.

When Terrence went back to the vet he had plenty of money with him. But he kept hoping that somehow Dr. Landis would say, "Since you're so kind, you don't have to pay."

Dr. Landis took him back to where the animals were kept in cages. There was the pigeon, looking as healthy as any pigeon.

Dr. Landis took it out of the cage. Then they went out through the back door, and Dr. Landis set the pigeon down gently on the ground.

Terrence half expected the pigeon to thank them somehow. But it just fluttered its wings and flew up to a window ledge.

Terrence reached for his wallet.

"That will be forty dollars," Dr. Landis said.

Terrence counted out the money. Then he looked for the pigeon. But it had flown out of sight.

The Lottery

by Shirley Jackson

You might not believe the story you are about to hear! You'll probably want me to read it again—because you won't believe what happens. Listen carefully. And then think, "Could this possibly happen here?"

The morning of June 27th was clear and sunny, with the fresh warmth of a full-summer day; the flowers were blossoming profusely and the grass was richly green. The people of the village began to gather in the square, between the post office and the bank, around ten o'clock; in some towns there were so many people that the lottery took two days and had to be started on June 26th, but in this village, where there were only about three hundred people, the whole lottery took less than two hours, so it could begin at ten o'clock in the morning and still be through in time to allow the villagers to get home for noon dinner.

The children assembled first, of course. School was recently over for the summer, and the feeling of liberty sat uneasily on most of them; they tended to gather together quietly for a while before they broke into boisterous play, and their talk was still of the classroom and the teacher, of books and reprimands. Bobby Martin had already stuffed his pockets full of stones, and the other boys soon followed his example, selecting the smoothest and roundest stones; Bobby and Harry Jones and Dickie Delacroix— the villagers pronounced this name "Dellacroy"—eventually made a great pile of stones in one corner of the square and guarded it against the raids of the other boys. The girls stood aside, talking among themselves, looking over their shoulders at the boys, and the very small children rolled in the dust or clung to the hands of their oldest brothers or sisters.

Soon the men began to gather, surveying their own children, speaking of planting and rain, tractors and taxes. They stood together, away from the pile of stones in the corner, and their jokes were quiet and they smiled rather than laughed. The women, wearing faded house dresses and sweaters, came shortly after their menfolk. They greeted one another and exchanged bits of gossip as they went to join their husbands. Soon the women, standing by their husbands, began to call to their children, and the children came reluctantly, having to be called four or five times. Bobby Martin ducked under his mother's grasping hand

and ran, laughing, back to the pile of stones. His father spoke up sharply, and Bobby came quickly and took his place between his father and his oldest brother.

The lottery was conducted—as were the square dances, the teen-age club, the Halloween program—by Mr. Summers, who had time and energy to devote to civic activities. He was a round-faced, jovial man and he ran the coal business, and people were sorry for him, because he had no children and his wife was a scold. When he arrived in the square, carrying the black wooden box, there was a murmur of conversation among the villagers, and he waved and called, "Little late today, folks." The postmaster, Mr. Graves, followed him, carrying a three-legged stool, and the stool was put in the center of the square and Mr. Summers set the black box down on it. The villagers kept their distance, leaving a space between themselves and the stool, and when Mr. Summers said, "Some of you fellows want to give me hand?" There was a hesitation before two men, Mr. Martin and his oldest son, Baxter, came forward to hold the box steady on the stool while Mr. Summers stirred up the papers inside it.

✳

The original paraphernalia for the lottery had been lost long ago, and the black box now resting on the stool had been put into use even before Old Man Warner, the oldest man in town, was born. Mr. Summers spoke frequently to the villagers about making a new box, but no one liked to upset even as much tradition as was represented by the black box. There was a story that the present box had been made with some pieces of the box that had preceded it, the one that had been constructed when the first people settled down to make a village here. Every year, after the lottery, Mr. Summers began talking again about a new box, but every year the subject was allowed to fade off without anything's being done. The black box grew shabbier each year; by now it was no longer completely black but splintered badly along one side to show original wood color, and in some places faded or stained.

Mr. Martin and his oldest son, Baxter, held the black box securely on the stool until Mr. Summers had stirred the papers thoroughly with his hand. Because so much of the ritual had been forgotten or discarded, Mr. Summers had been successful in having slips of paper substituted for the chips of wood that had been used for generations. Chips of wood, Mr. Summers had argued, had been all very well when the village was tiny, but now that the population was more than three hundred and likely to keep on growing, it was necessary to use something that would fit more easily into the black box. The night before the lottery, Mr. Summers and Mr. Graves made up the slips of paper and put them in the box, and it was then taken to the safe of Mr. Summers' coal company and locked up until Mr. Summers was ready to take it to the square next morning. The rest of the year, the box was put away, sometimes one place, sometimes another; it had spent one year in Mr. Graves's barn and another year underfoot in the post office, and sometimes it was set on a shelf in the Martin grocery and left there.

There was a great deal of fussing to be done before Mr. Summer declared the lottery open. There were the lists to make up—of heads of families, heads of households in each family, members of each household in each family. There was the proper swearing-in of Mr. Summers by the postmaster, as the official of the lottery; at one time, some people remembered, there had been a recital of some sort, performed by the official of the lottery, a perfunctory, tuneless chant that had been rattled off duly each year; some people believed that the official of the lottery used to stand just so when he said or sang it, others believed that he was supposed to walk among the people, but years and years ago this part of the ritual had been allowed to lapse. There had been, also, a ritual salute, which the official of the lottery had had to use in addressing each person who came up to draw from the box, but this also had changed with time, until now it was felt necessary only for the official to speak to each person approaching. Mr. Summers was very good at all this; in his clean white shirts and blue jeans, with one hand resting carelessly on the black box, he seemed very proper and important as he talked interminably to Mr. Graves and the Martins.

Just as Mr. Summers finally left off talking and turned to the assembled villagers, Mrs. Hutchinson came hurriedly along the path to the square, her sweater thrown over her shoulders, and slid into place in the back of the crowd. "Clean forgot what day it was," she said to Mrs. Delacroix, who stood next to her, and they both laughed softly. "Thought my old man was out back stacking wood," Mrs. Hutchinson went on, "and then I looked out the window and the kids was gone,

and I remembered it was the twenty-seventh and came-a-running." She dried her hands on her apron, and Mrs. Delacroix said, "You're in time, though. They're still talking away up there."

※

Mrs. Hutchinson craned her neck to see through the crowd and found her husband and children standing near the front. She tapped Mrs. Delacroix on the arm as a farewell and began to make her way through the crowd. The people separated good-humoredly to let her through; two or three people said, in voices just loud enough to be heard across the crowd, "Here comes your Missus, Hutchinson," and "Bill, she made it after all."

Mrs. Hutchinson reached her husband, and Mr. Summers, who had been waiting, said cheerfully, "Thought we were going to have to get on without you, Tessie." Mrs. Hutchinson said, grinning, "Wouldn't have me leave m'dishes in the sink, now, would you, Joe?" and soft laughter ran through the crowd as the people stirred back into position after Mrs. Hutchinson's arrival.

"Well, now," Mr. Summers said soberly, "guess we better get started, get this over with, so's we can go back to work. Anybody ain't here?"

"Dunbar," several people said. "Dunbar, Dunbar."

Mr. Summers consulted his list. "Clyde Dunbar," he said. "That's right. He's broke his leg, hasn't he? Who's drawing for him?"

"Me, I guess," a woman said, and Mr. Summers turned to look at her. "Wife draws for her husband," Mr. Summers said. "Don't you have a grown boy to do it for you, Janey?" Although Mr. Summers and everyone else in the village knew the answer perfectly well, it was the business of the official of the lottery to ask such questions formally. Mr. Summers waited with an expression of polite interest while Mrs. Dunbar answered.

"Horace's not but sixteen yet," Mrs. Dunbar said regretfully. "Guess I gotta fill in for the old man this year."

"Right," Mr. Summers said. He made a note on the list he was holding. Then he asked, "Watson boy drawing this year?"

A tall boy in the crowd raised his hand. "Here," he said. "I'm drawing for m'mother and me." He blinked his eyes nervously and ducked his head as several voices in the crowd said things like "Good fellow, Jack," and "Glad to see your mother's got a man to do it."

"Well," Mr. Summers said, "guess that's everyone. Old Man Warner make it?"

"Here," a voice said, and Mr. Summers nodded.

A sudden hush fell on the crowd as Mr. Summers cleared his throat and looked at the list. "All ready?" he called. "Now, I'll read the names—heads of families first—and the men come up and take a paper out of the box. Keep the paper folded in your hand without looking at it until everyone has had a turn. Everything clear?"

The people had done it so many times that they only half listened to the directions; most of them were quiet, wetting their lips, not looking around.

Then Mr. Summers raised one hand high and said, "Adams." A man disengaged himself from the crowd and came forward. "Hi, Steve," Mr. Summers said, and Mr. Adams said, "Hi, Joe." They grinned at one another humorously and nervously. Then Mr. Adams reached into the black box and took out a folded paper. He held if firmly by one corner as he turned and went hastily back to his place in the crowd, where he stood a little apart from his family, not looking down at his hand.

"Allen," Mr. Summers said. "Anderson . . . Bentham."

"Seems like there's no time at all between lotteries any more," Mrs. Delacroix said to Mrs. Graves in the back row. "Seems like we got through with the last one only last week."

"Time sure goes fast," Mrs. Graves said.

"Clark . . . Delacroix."

"There goes my old man," Mrs. Delacroix said. She held her breath while her husband went forward.

"Dunbar," Mr. Summers said, and Mrs. Dunbar went steadily to the box while one of the woman said, "Go on, Janey," and another said, "There she goes."

"We're next," Mrs. Graves said. She watched while Mr. Graves came around from the side of the box, greeted Mr. Summers gravely, and selected a slip of paper from the box. By now, all through the crowd there were men holding the small folded papers in their large hands, turning them over and over nervously. Mrs. Dunbar and her two sons stood together, Mrs. Dunbar holding the slip of paper.

"Harburt . . . Hutchinson."

"Get up there, Bill," Mrs. Hutchinson said, and the people near her laughed.

"Jones."

"They do say," Mr. Adams said to Old Man Warner, who stood next to him, "that over in the north village they're talking of giving up the lottery."

Old Man Warner snorted. "Pack of crazy fools," he said. "Listening to the young folks, nothing's good enough for them. Next thing you know, they'll be wanting to go back to living in caves, nobody work any more, live *that* way for a while. Used to be a saying about 'Lottery in June, corn be heavy soon.' First thing you know, we'd all be eating stewed chickweed and acorns. There's always been a lottery," he added petulantly. "Bad enough to see young Joe Summers up there joking with everybody."

"Some places have already quit lotteries," Mrs. Adams said.

"Nothing but trouble in *that*," Old Man Warner said stoutly. "Pack of young fools."

"Martin." And Bobby Martin watched his father go forward. "Overdyke...Percy."

"I wish they'd hurry," Mrs. Dunbar said to her older son. "I wish they'd hurry."

"They're almost through," her son said.

"You get ready to run to tell Dad," Mrs. Dunbar said.

Mr. Summers called his own name and then stepped forward precisely and selected a slip from the box. Then he called, "Warner."

"Seventy-seventh year I been in the lottery," Old Man Warner said as he went through the crowd. "Seventy-seventh time."

"Watson." The tall boy came awkwardly through the crowd. Someone said, "Don't be nervous, Jack," and Mr. Summers said, "Take your time, son."

"Zanini."

After that, there was a long pause, a breathless pause, until Mr. Summers, holding his slip of paper in the air, said, "All right, fellows." For a minute, no one moved, and then all the slips of papers were opened. Suddenly, all the women began to speak at once, saying, "Who is it?," "Who's got it?," "Is it the Dunbars?," "Is it the Watsons?," Then the voices began to say, "It's Hutchinson. It's Bill," "Bill Hutchinson's got it."

"Go tell your father," Mrs. Dunbar said to her older son.

✳

People began to look around to see the Hutchinsons. Bill Hutchinson was standing quiet, staring down at the paper in his hand. Suddenly, Tessie Hutchinson shouted to Mr. Summers, "You didn't give him time enough to take any paper he wanted. I saw you. It wasn't fair!"

"Be a good sport, Tessie," Mrs. Delacroix called, and Mrs. Graves said, "All of us took the same chance."

"Shut up, Tessie," Bill Hutchinson said.

"Well, everyone," Mr. Summers said, "that was done pretty fast, and now we've got to be hurrying a little more to get done in time." He consulted his next list. "Bill," he said, "you draw for the Hutchinson family. You got any other household in the Hutchinsons?"

"There's Don and Eva," Mrs. Hutchinson yelled. "Make *them* take their chance!"

"Daughters draw with their husbands' families, Tessie," Mr. Summers said gently. "You know that as well as anyone else."

"It wasn't *fair*," Tessie said.

"I guess not, Joe," Bill Hutchinson said regretfully. "My daughter draws with her husband's family, that's only fair. And I've got no other family except the kids."

"Then, as far as drawing for families is concerned, it's you," Mr. Summers said in explanation, "and as far as drawing for households is concerned, that's you, too. Right?"

"Right," Bill Hutchinson said.

"How many kids, Bill?" Mr. Summers asked formally.

"Three," Bill Hutchinson said. "There's Bill, Jr., and Nancy, and little Dave. And Tessie and me."

"All right, then," Mr. Summers said. "Harry, you got their tickets back?"

Mr. Graves nodded and held up the slips of paper. "Put them in the box, then," Mr. Summers directed. "Take Bill's and put it in."

"I think we ought to start over," Mrs. Hutchinson said, as quietly as she could.

"I tell you it wasn't *fair*. You didn't give him time enough to choose. Everybody saw that."

Mr. Graves had selected the five slips and put them in the ground, where the breeze caught them and lifted them off.

"Listen, everybody," Mrs. Hutchinson was saying to the people around her.

"Ready, Bill?" Mr. Summers asked, and Bill Hutchinson, with one quick glance around at his wife and children, nodded.

"Remember," Mr. Summers said, "take the slips and keep them folded until each person has taken one. Harry, you help little Dave." Mr. Graves took the hand of the little boy, who came willingly with him to the box. "Take a paper out of the box, Davy," Mr. Summers said. Davy put his hand into the box and laughed. "Take just one paper," Mr. Summers said. "Harry, you hold it for him." Mr. Graves took the child's hand and removed the folded paper from the tight fist and held it while little Dave stood next to him and looked up at him wonderingly.

"Nancy next," Mr. Summers said. Nancy was twelve, and her school friends breathed heavily as she went forward, switching her skirt, and took a slip daintily from the box. "Bill, Jr.," Mr. Summers said, and Billy, his face red and his feet over-large, nearly knocked the box over as he got a paper out. "Tessie," Mr. Summers said. She hesitated for a minute, looking around defiantly, and then set her lips and went up to the box. She snatched a paper out and held it behind her.

"Bill," Mr. Summers said, and Bill Hutchinson reached into the box and felt around, bringing his hand out at last with the slip of paper in it.

The crowd was quiet. A girl whispered, "I hope it's not Nancy," and the sound of the whisper reached the edges of the crowd.

"It's not the way it used to be," Old Man Warner said clearly. "People ain't the way they used to be."

"All right," Mr. Summers said. "Open the papers. Harry, you open little Dave's."

Mr. Graves opened the slip of paper and there was a general sigh through the crowd as he held it up and everyone could see that it was blank. Nancy and Bill, Jr., opened theirs at the same time, and both beamed and laughed, turning around to the crowd while holding their slips of papers above their heads.

"Tessie," Mr. Summers said. There was a pause, and then Mr. Summers looked at Bill Hutchinson, and Bill unfolded his paper and showed it. It was blank.

"It's Tessie," Mr. Summers said, and his voice was hushed.

"Show us her paper, Bill."

✳

Bill Hutchinson went over to his wife and forced the slip of paper out of her hand. It had a black spot on it, the black spot Mr. Summers had made the night before with the heavy pencil in the coal-company office. Bill Hutchinson held it up, and there was a stir in the crowd.

"All right, folks," Mr. Summers said. "Let's finish quickly."

Although the villagers had forgotten the ritual and lost the original black box, they still remembered to use stones. The pile of stones the boys had made earlier was ready; there were stones on the ground with the blowing scraps of paper that had come out of the box. Mrs. Delacroix selected a stone so large she had to pick it up with both hands and turned to Mrs. Dunbar. "Come on," she said. "Hurry up."

Mrs. Dunbar had small stones in both hands, and she said, gasping for breath, "I can't run at all. You'll have to go ahead and I'll catch up with you."

The children had stones already, and someone gave little Dave Hutchinson a few pebbles.

Tessie Hutchinson was in the center of a cleared space by now, and she held her hands out desperately as the villagers moved in on her. "It isn't fair," she said. A stone hit her on the side of the head.

Old Man Warner was saying, "Come on, come on, everyone." Steve Adams was in the front of the crowd of villagers, with Mrs. Graves beside him.

"It isn't fair, it isn't right," Mrs. Hutchinson screamed, and then they were upon her.

Romeo and Juliet at the Mall

Do you hate the idea of reading Shakespeare? Do you feel like Shakespeare is just too hard to understand? Maybe it would be easier to understand if it was retold differently. Maybe it would be easier to understand if you heard it through the eyes of an American teenager. So, imagine that you are sitting at the food court in the local mall. And you are listening to some kid retell this classic love story. See if it makes more sense to you now.

Like this is a totally sad play. This guy Shakespeare must have really wanted to get the girls—and a few dudes—crying at the end. Because, trust me, there's no happy ending here. Here's how it goes.

There is this dude Romeo—he's fierce. And then there's this hottie—Juliet. They had names like that 'cause it was like the really old days, even way before MTV. So, no one had cool names like Carson, Britney, or J Lo. They all had really geeky names like Benvolio and Tybalt and Mercutio.

They come from these two huge families with like tons of cousins and second cousins. One family is the Montagues and the other is the Capulets. And, man, they really hate each other. I mean, they can't even walk down the street without wailing on each other. And that's what happens right at the beginning of the story.

This dude, Sampson, who works for old man Capulet, sees this other dude, Abraham, who hangs with a Montague, and he bites his thumb. I mean, like, Sampson bites his own thumb, not Abraham's thumb, which in the old days was like saying "Wanna fight?"

And Abraham says something like, "Do *you* wanna fight?" So they both start beatin' on each other. But it gets broken up before anybody's really messed up, you know. And the Prince—he's like the principal of this whole town—he says, "Yo, next time you guys get in each other's face, I'm gonna twist someone's head around so their cap's on straight."

So, back to the story. Remember Juliet? She's the cute one. Well her old man decides he's going to have this kickin' party. But he has to send this servant out to tell everybody, 'cause, like, they didn't have cell phones or beepers then. But this servant is like a little slow or something, and he can't make out the names on the list, so he stops someone to help him read it. And check it out—it's Romeo.

So Romeo looks at the list, and there's all these names of people he doesn't really like. But then he sees Rosaline's name. She's this chick who is like totally hot and Romeo has always wanted to date her. So he decides to crash the party, which is easy, see 'cause it's a masquerade party.

Meanwhile, Juliet's mom, she's trying to fix Juliet up with this guy named Paris. Whatever.

Anyway, Romeo's kind of bummed because he is totally into Rosaline and he thinks she, like, isn't into him. But one of Romeo's buds, Mercutio, tells him, like, "Chill. Ro-boy. Just go to the party and hang out. There's going to be like a lot of girls there."

So Romeo goes to the party. He's checking out the girls. Nobody really makes him look twice. That is till he sees Juliet! And he goes, HELLO!, "Who is that totally crushable babe?" And at the same time she's saying to herself, "Who is that major cutie?" Which is bad, see, 'cause like, in the beginning of the story, Shakespeare, already said that Romeo and Juliet were "star cross'd lovers," which probably means this relationship is totally doomed anyway.

But that doesn't stop them. So Romeo goes up and busts a move, and they hold hands for a while. Then he gets some nerve and he goes, "O, then, dear saint, let lips do what hands do." And he kisses her, and it's like, *Wow*! I mean it was totally awesome for both of them. But then Juliet's nurse pulls her away. In those days a nurse was like a nanny for older girls. And they were always going

completely ballistic over nothing—but especially kissing.

Juliet's cousin, Tybalt, sees that Romeo is trying to ease in on Juliet. And since she is a Capulet and Romeo is a Montague, there is no way he is going to let this happen. So he says, "Yo, hand me that sword." But Juliet's dad says, "Chill. Don't wreck the party."

Then it's curfew time or something 'cause everyone has to leave, but when Romeo is heading for his part of town, he stops, and jumps over this big fence into Juliet's yard. He's like climbing up trees to get near Juliet's bedroom. At the same time Juliet goes out to her balcony and kind of stares up at the moon. She gets all goofy and says, "O, Romeo, Romeo, wherefore art thou Romeo?" And it's like, HELLO!, he's sitting on a branch right under her balcony. But maybe, like, she took her contacts out to go to bed.

But she figures it out, and suddenly Romeo's climbing up the wall cause he wants to hang with his honey on the balcony. He's not there but for only a minute when, Boom!, they fall in love. I mean, they have it so bad for each other that Romeo goes, "Do you want to get married?" And she goes, "Yeah, that would be excellent!" So they run off and get married. Only they get married in secret because remember, their families hate each other.

But then, like, right after this, Juliet's pushy cousin Tybalt shows up again and starts getting in Romeo's face. See he doesn't know they're married cause he didn't get an invitation. And, like, he should be happy because he didn't have to buy a present or anything. But he wants to kill Romeo. I mean, he's flipping out. (Nice, eh?) But Romeo won't fight him, so Tybalt jumps in Mercutio's face, and he and Mercutio start beating on each other. Mercutio gets killed, so Romeo kills Tybalt, which is dumb, 'cause now he and Juliet definitely aren't gonna be getting any wedding presents from either side of the family.

Then the prince exiles Romeo, which is like being expelled from school, but you've got to go to a whole other state or something. So Romeo and Juliet have to split for a while. Juliet goes, "O, think'st thou we shall ever meet again?" cause she's really in love and is afraid that Romeo won't be able to come back. And then Juliet starts bummin' even more 'cause now her old man wants her to marry Paris. EXCUSE ME! She's like already married. But her parents are clueless about that and are still planning a wedding, so it looks like she's going to get presents one way or another. But then this priest guy gives Juliet this stuff to drink so that everyone will think she's dead, until Romeo can get back from being grounded. But this stuff is so good that everybody thinks she really is dead, and they put her in this tomb thing.

Then Romeo dreams Juliet has found him dead, and even though he's grounded in another state, he says, "Later. I'm outta here." He takes off to see Juliet, but he stops, like at a drugstore for some poison. So he misses this letter that the priest sent that says, "Juliet isn't dead. She's just sleeping." Ooops.

But then Romeo sees Juliet and he goes, "Ah, dear Juliet, why art thou yet so fair?" 'Cause, you know, if she was dead she ought to be green and starting to smell funny. And that totally bums him

out, so he takes the poison. *Duh!* I mean, *Duhh!* Then you'll never guess this part. She wakes up and sees Romeo and goes, "O happy dagger!" and kills herself.

I mean, are these people for real, or, like, what?

And that's Shakespeare's most famous love story.

Pictures of You

by Guang-Shing Cheng

Guang-Shing was a student at Winston Churchill High School in Potomac, Maryland, when she wrote this letter to her brother. However, her brother will never receive the letter. Guang's brother was killed in a terrible accident when he was nine and she was only five. "Writing this letter," explained Guang-Shing, "is like a tribute to my older brother." She said it also helped to heal the sadness that she's always felt—and could never talk about. Here is Guang-Shing's letter

Dear Brother,

Dad caught me in the closet looking at the old photo albums. I was sitting there, with the album in my lap opened to the picture of you and me and Mom on a bed giggling. When dad opened the door, I tried to hide my face among the hanging clothes, but I'm sure he noticed my hot, puffy eyes and said that he and Mom were trying to sleep, so I left, taking the albums in which we are together. Well, Dad noticed that too, so he followed me to my room. Thank God, I locked the door in time.

Then he knocked on my door and said, "Don't look at those pictures now." And as an afterthought, "It's late." Come to think of it, I'm the only one now who ever looks at those pictures. Since you left, there have been albums and albums of me and Ien (our little brother) and Mom and Dad, but there are only three with pictures of you. These I always have to get out from under all the rest.

The pictures are mostly of the mountains, remember? There are pictures of Yellowstone and Mount Rushmore, where you found the smelly remains of a mountain goat that was probably eaten by a mountain lion. I remember that you were the only one of us who dared to go near the formidable pile of bones and shreds of clinging meat that seemed to reach for me. My four-year-old mind couldn't accept how a nice cute goat could die and become a gross, skeletal monster.

Well, it's been 12 years since that vacation. Time has a funny way of twisting my perception of you. You'll always be my big brother, although you will never grow out of your nine-year-old body. Did you know that I dreaded turning nine, because I thought I would die, too? I wonder if you are still nine in soul or 20, like you would be if you were still here. Can you hear me and know what I'm feeling? Maybe time has made you ageless.

Eleven years since I saw you. Today we are the average American family, Mom and Dad, two kids. It's just Ien and me now. When I look at the photo albums filled after you went away, I wonder what they would look like with you there, hugging me and tousling Ien's hair. If you were here, our round breakfast table might not be so symmetrical. It would be a tighter squeeze, but I wouldn't mind.

You know, if you were here, you'd live in the room across from me where all the guests stay. This year you'd probably be at college, somewhere like Harvard. Mom and Dad would be even tighter with the checkbook than they are now, but I wouldn't mind. Maybe you'd come home with a girlfriend or some tall dark handsome friend who would say, "So you're the strange kid sister Guang-Yeu's been bragging about." I would be able to tell all my friends about the crazy things my 20-year-old brother does. You could drive me to school and even sign sick notes for me when I was really sleeping in, since you would have gone through it all before me. I'm sure you would yell at me for constantly "borrowing" your stuff, but you'd still tease me and play stupid card games with me. Maybe I wouldn't have had such a hard time with Mom and Dad about doing things. And you'd be in the pictures of our family outings.

Maybe you would be none of these things; I'll never know. I do know that if you hadn't left, we wouldn't have to talk about you in hushed tones and act like there was always the four of us, the ever-so-happy average American family.

We moved after you left. Mom couldn't bear to live on the street where the accident occurred. I don't think Mom and Dad kept in touch with anyone from that neighborhood after you left. For months it

seemed like Mom cried, or actually flooded, the house with her sobs. If I mentioned your name, she would break down. After a while I just didn't mention you at all.

Even today, whenever my friends come over and they ask who drew your "Monster Feature" poster that hangs in the kitchen, I always respond a little haltingly, "Oh, that. A distant cousin drew it." I did tell someone once, a short while after you left. At the time I didn't understand why Mom and Dad were so upset that I told: I was only five. Once I understood that you weren't coming back, I couldn't tell people "My big brother drew that" and explain you without feeling red and blue and puffy.

Did I already mention that I'm the only one who ever looks at the albums? Sometimes I ask Mom if she'd like to look at them with me and she'll absent-mindedly say OK, we should. Then I'll ask if Ien and I were pretty babies and she says yes, we were, but you were the prettiest of the three. I guess Mom doesn't need photos to see your baby face. And you know how close-lipped Dad is about these things. He has a picture of you wrapped in yellowing plastic, an eternally preserved taboo, but he doesn't like looking at old photos. I always end up looking at the albums alone, so I can remember your face.

Most of the time, we live as if you were never with us, and I was always the oldest child in the family. Mom doesn't cry anymore. Sometimes she'll mention you, though not in a sad way. Dad never mentions you, except when we visit your grave. Ien never mentions you.

As for me, I have to tell people who

have older brothers how lucky they are. I can only imagine what life would be like now, if you were here. I have wanted to ask our parents what you were like, since I was too young when you left to remember much about you. I have wanted to tell people what "death at an early age" is really like. This is the best way I know how.

Are you happier where you are now than when you were here? Don't you miss being able to grow up with us and doing those things that you could be doing? You left me with what some may call grief, or sorrow, or mourning, but there is no word to describe it. It is the feeling that makes me cry in the dark when I'm alone, and ask these questions, knowing that you won't answer.

Sometimes I feel as if I am a stranger looking at those pictures, that those cute kids couldn't have been you and me and Ien. It's been a long time since I've seen you. If I reach into the recesses of my memory, I can catch glimpses of you leading me, carrying me. Each year the pictures mean more to me because those images of you are fading. Every time I look at them, I cry for being too young to know you other than as a big person that I could cling to. I also cry for a hopeless vision of what life could be, should be, if you were here. The pictures are the only things I have left of you, so I at least know that you once held me in your nine-year-old arms.

The Open Window

by Saki

In this classic story you are about to meet Framton Nuttel, who is trying to get acquainted with some of his neighbors. Poor Mr. Nuttel . . . he came to the country for relaxation and to calm his nervous condition. Unfortunately, he's about to witness an extraordinary—and very unnerving—event. Would you be as unnerved as Mr. Nuttel gets?

"My aunt will be down soon," said the 15-year-old girl. "While you wait, you must put up with me."

Framton Nuttel tried to find the right thing to say. He should be polite, of course, but he should seem to want to meet the aunt very much.

Framton was in the country to cure his nerves. His sister had wanted him to meet some people she knew there. "If you don't speak to anyone, your nerves will be worse than ever," she had told him, "and some of these people are very nice." Framton didn't think that visits to strangers would help him much. He hoped that Mrs. Sappleton, the aunt, was one of the "nice" ones.

"Do you know very many people around here?" the niece asked.

"Hardly anybody," said Framton. "My sister stayed with friends here about four years ago. She wanted me to meet some people she liked."

"Then you know almost nothing about my aunt," said the girl.

"Only her name and address," said Framton. He wondered if Mrs. Sappleton was married or a widow. Something about the room made him think that a man lived there.

"The most terrible thing happened to her three years ago," said the girl. "It was not long after your sister was here."

"A terrible thing?" asked Framton. Terrible things seemed unlikely in this quiet country spot.

"You may be wondering why we keep that window wide open on an October afternoon," said the niece. She pointed to a large French window that opened onto a rolling green lawn.

"It's warm for this time of year," said Framton, "but does that window have anything to do with the terrible thing?"

"It all started when they went out through that window, three years ago today," the girl said mysteriously. "My aunt's husband and her two young brothers were going hunting with their little brown dog. None of them ever came back. They must have slipped into a swamp and drowned. The worst part was that their bodies were never found." Here the girl's voice started to crack. "My poor aunt! She believes that they will walk in through that window, just like they used to. That's why she keeps the window open."

"My poor, dear aunt. She always talks about the way they went out. Her husband had his red coat over is arm. Ronnie, her younger brother, was singing an old song, 'My Bonnie Lies Over the Ocean.' He did that to tease her—it got on her nerves. You know, sometimes, on a still, quiet evening like this, I get a creepy feeling. I almost think they will all walk in through that window . . . "

She broke off, shaking her head. Framton was glad when the aunt came into the room, saying how sorry she was to be late.

"I hope you have enjoyed talking to Vera," she said.

"She has been very interesting," said Framton.

"I hope you don't mind the open window," said Mrs. Sappleton. "My husband and brothers will be home soon. They've been hunting, and they always come in this way. They'll have shot some birds, so they'll mess up the rug, but that's the way men are, isn't it?"

She chattered on cheerfully. She talked about hunting, and how it might be better next winter. To Framton, it was awful. He saw that Vera's aunt was not paying much attention to him. Her eyes were on the open window and the lawn. He was sorry that he had come to visit on this, of all days.

"The doctors say I should do nothing exciting and get lots of rest," Framton said, trying to change the subject. He had not yet learned that few people are interested in other people's health. "Of course, none of them agree about what I should eat."

"No?" said Mrs. Sappleton. Then her face grew brighter, but it was not because of their conversation.

"Here they are at last!" she cried. "They're just in time for tea. They look as if they were muddy right up to their eyeballs!"

Framton turned toward the niece, to give her an understanding look, but the girl was staring out through the open window. Her eyes filled wide with fear.

In the gray light, three figures were walking across the lawn toward the window. They were carrying guns under their arms. One of them had a red coat over his shoulders. A tired brown dog followed close behind. They drew near the house without making a sound, but suddenly a young voice began to sing, "My Bonnie lies over the ocean . . . "

Framton jumped to his feet and ran for the door. Out in the road, a man on a bicycle had to run into a hedge to keep from running into him.

"Here we are, dear," said the man with the red coat, coming in through the window. "We're muddy, but most of it's dry. Who was that who ran out as we came up?"

"A very strange man, a Mr. Nuttel," said Mrs. Sappleton. "He only talked about being ill. Then he ran off without saying good-bye. You'd think he had seen a ghost."

"It was probably the dog," said Vera. "He told me he was afraid of dogs and that once he was chased into a graveyard in India by a pack of wild dogs. He had to spend the night in a grave that had just been dug, and the dogs barked and howled and snapped right above him all night. I'm sure it was enough to make anyone lose their nerve."

Making up exciting stories on short notice was Vera's specialty.

The Sound of Annie's Silence

by Phyllis Fair Cowell

If you answered an ad for a babysitting job, you'd probably expect to take care of one or two kids for a few hours or so, right? Well, that's what the girl in this story thinks, too. But this is no ordinary babysitting job. And, Annie, the girl who is being taken care of, is no ordinary girl. And soon the sitter realizes that people have feelings—even when they can't say them aloud.

When I answered the ad, I had no idea what I was getting into. It sounded simple enough.

Wanted: Someone to stay with my daughter Mon.-Fri. afternoons 3:30 – 5:30. High school student preferred. $25/wk.

I called the number listed with the ad. The next day I met Mrs. Walters and her daughter, Annie.

Meeting Annie was a shock. Mrs. Walters led me to a girl sitting in the living room. I stood there, staring.

The girl I was supposed to watch was no child at all. Annie was my age!

"Hello," I finally muttered.

"Annie doesn't talk," Mrs. Walters said.

I realized that Annie was staring, too, but not at me. I wasn't sure if she was really looking at anything. I couldn't even tell if she knew I was there.

"What's wrong with her?" I asked.

Mrs. Walter tried to explain, but the long words were lost on me. I did understand that Annie went to a special school. In a few months, she would go live there. Until then, Mrs. Walters needed help with Annie.

"Someone has to watch Annie until I get home from work," she explained. "She likes being around people her own age. So I thought a student would be good for the job. Are you still interested?"

I thought for a second. Annie didn't seem to do much of anything. Watching her would be easier than babysitting.

"Sure," I said.

Mrs. Walters described the job. I would pick up the house keys at a neighbor's house. Annie's school bus would bring her home by 3:45. All I had to do was watch Annie until Mrs. Walters got home. If I had any problems, I could call on the neighbor for help.

I couldn't believe it. I could study or watch TV—and get paid for it. The job would be a breeze.

That's what I thought then.

That was before I heard the sound of Annie's silence.

I can't say just what it was like. At first I thought she was watching me. That was silly. Annie stared, but I never knew what she saw with those eyes. It made it hard to ignore her.

I began doing things for her. I put her chair next to a window so she could stare at different things. I turned on the TV for her. Mostly, though, I tried not to think about her.

Annie had her good days and her bad days. On good days, she just sat. On bad days, she rocked back and forth. The chair legs would slam on the floor. Annie's head would bang on the wall behind her.

On one of Annie's bad days, I started talking to her. "Come on, Annie!" I said crossly, "Cut it out!"

I slammed my history book shut, but Annie kept rocking. I moved her away from the wall so she wouldn't hurt her head.

The rocking stopped. Now there was her silence again—and her staring. That was almost worse than the rocking and the banging. Suddenly, I couldn't stand it any longer. I grabbed my jacket and headed for the door.

Then I realized I couldn't just leave Annie there. But I had to get away from the walls that echoed her silence.

I shoved Annie's arms into her coat, and I pulled her outside with me. As soon as Mrs. Walters got home, I decided, I was going to quit this crazy job.

Crazy was the word for it. Here I was, trying to get away from Annie. But instead, I was walking with her, and I was even holding her hand. I had to. If I didn't she would just stand there.

Crazier than that, I was still talking to her. "It's much better out here, isn't it?" I asked. Even though I knew she couldn't answer, I went on. "There's a lot more to see here than indoors. That's the new playground over there. And over there is the corner where I catch my bus home."

We got back to the house late. Mrs. Walters was already home. I wanted to tell her I was quitting, but she started talking first.

"It was so nice of you to take Annie for a walk," she said. "You don't have to do that, you know. You're so good with her. I appreciate that."

She kept saying things that made it hard to quit right then. I decided to quit the next day.

The next day came and went, and I said nothing about quitting. The whole week went by without my bringing it up.

Almost every day, I took Annie for a walk. If the weather was bad, I sat and looked out the window with her. All the time, I kept talking to her. It made her silence easier to bear.

I pointed out cars and people and buses. I talked about trees, birds, and even umbrellas. Every day I thought about quitting, but I did nothing about it.

My last day of work finally arrived. Annie would begin living at her school from now on. I could tell Mrs. Walters was sad that Annie was moving away, but she tried not to show it.

"Annie's school runs a day camp during the summer," she told me. "They hire teenagers to help out. I've told them about you, and I'm sure you could get a job there."

Oh, no, I thought. I don't want to work with a lot of Annies.

Out loud I said, "Thank you, Mrs. Walters, but I already have a summer job." That was a lie.

When I left the house, I felt relieved. But I didn't feel as happy as I thought I would. When I missed my bus, I didn't care, I just felt numb.

I stood at the bus stop, wondering why I felt so bad. I had said good-bye to Annie quickly and without emotion. Then I had left as fast as I could.

Now I tried to look for something to cheer me up. I noticed the kids in the playground across the street. They all seemed happy—except for one girl. She was older than the others, and she stood outside the playground.

When I looked at her closely, I could see it was Annie. As I ran toward her, I wondered how she had gotten outside. She had never wandered away before. Maybe she felt my good-bye wasn't enough.

I threw my arms around her and gave her a hug. Then I took her hand, and we headed back to the house.

I began to feel happier. I knew what I would be doing this summer. My job with Annie hadn't been so bad, once I started treating her like the human being she was.

Dumb Crimes and Dumber Criminals!

by Denise Rinaldo

We all know that crime doesn't pay. Most criminals end up behind bars because of good detective work. Even the really, really smart ones get caught. But sometimes the criminals just make it easy! These two crime capers I'm going to read are about dumb criminals and the really dumb mistakes that got them caught!

This first one is called the case of the sloppy shoplifter!

While browsing at a trendy clothing store, 19-year-old Jonathan Parker realized that he really wanted a leather jacket. Then, he realized that he wouldn't be happy with just one! Jonathan wanted three leather jackets! Of course, he didn't have any money. So he had no choice but to take a "five-finger discount." That is, he decided to steal them.

Jonathan surveyed the premises and saw the sensor alarm in front of the shop's exit. He knew the merchandise was tagged with magnetic strips; if he tried to slip out with any tagged merchandise, the sensor would set off a deafening siren.

Undaunted, Jonathan grabbed some jackets that suited his taste and ducked into the nearest dressing room. He searched the jackets, peeling off every one of the magnetic strips. He checked inside the sleeves and pockets, under the collars and along the waistbands. This clever criminal was very proud of himself as he flicked the last of the strips onto the floor. He carefully stuffed the jackets under his coat and boldly walked toward the front door.

Jonathan was just about to approach the sensor alarms, but he wasn't worried. He was confident that he had removed *every* magnetic strip. However, his confidence was shattered when the loud, piercing alarm went off. The noise alerted the security guard who quickly apprehended the young thief. Jonathan was stunned. What could have gone wrong?

As Jonathan sat in the security office waiting for the police to arrive, the security guard searched the stolen jackets. He found that Jonathan *had* really removed every single magnetic strip! So what set off the alarm?

The guard looked at the leather jackets. Then he looked at Jonathan. The guard noticed something sticking out from under Jonathan's shoe. When

Jonathan picked up his feet, the guard saw all the magnetic strips stuck there. Jonathan had thrown the sticky strips onto the floor and then stepped on them. The young man was arrested and charged with shoplifting.

The lesson here: sticky fingers and sticky shoes don't mix.

Now, here's another crime story that will really test your sensibilities! This one is called the case of the ridiculous robber.

Dwayne Carver was a maintenance man at the Cedar Wood Apartments in Virginia Beach, Virginia. He had a good job and his own tools. He even had a pretty cool blue uniform.

Dwayne decided to rob a 7-Eleven store. He had the robbery all planned out: he wore a ski mask to hide his face and a cap to hide his hair color. Dwayne even rented a car so that he couldn't be traced.

When he approached the clerk, his hair and face were completely covered. He deepened his voice so it could not be recognized. When he said, "Give me all the money," the startled clerk stared at Dwayne. He looked at the robber's mask and hat. Then he looked the robber up and down for a moment. Finally—smiling to himself—the clerk handed over the several hundred dollars that was in the register.

The police arrived shortly, and they asked the clerk to describe the robber. "I can't tell you much about what he looked like," the clerk explained. "He had a cap and a mask on, but I can tell you that his blue maintenance uniform said 'Cedar Wood Apartments' on the back and 'Dwayne' on the front."

The two officers figured the thief probably stole this uniform or bought it used at Goodwill, that *no* criminal would be dumb enough to wear his real uniform to a robbery. But, yes, Dwayne was that dumb.

When the officers appeared at Dwayne's apartment, he hadn't even changed clothes. The ski mask was in his back pocket. The gun was in his other back pocket. The money was in his front pocket. Case closed.

The lesson here: a uniform—with your name stitched on it—is probably not a good disguise.

Skunks: Sweet but Smelly

by Joy Masoff

Have you ever smelled the spray from a skunk? It is the king of all farts...an oily rear-end eruption so stinky that it'll make your nose want to close up shop and your eyes burn and water. You can even taste the foulness. And the bringer of all these bad tidings? A sweet, cuddly critter with a kind heart and two powerful stink-bomb glands next to its butt!

Skunks are actually pretty nice little stinkers. And when they are happy, they smell just fine. But they don't like being pushed around, and they don't like anything bigger than they are. (Unfortunately for our noses, lots of things are bigger than they are.) When skunks feel threatened, they have a not-so-secret weapon and they're not afraid to use it.

Let's say you're walking through the woods and you find yourself in a face-off with a skunk. Since you are a lot bigger than a skunk, the skunk naturally feels threatened. (Admit it. You'd feel that way too if you ran into someone who was 20 times taller than you.) The skunk hopes that you'll go away. Only problem is, you're too terrified to move.

The skunk stamps the ground with its feet. Its teeth may chatter. In skunk-talk, this all means "Get out of here, now, you idiot!" But, fool that you are, you stand there, feet still glued to the ground. So, the skunk moves on to phase two, raising its bushy tail. But the tip is still limp. What do you do? Quick! Run! There's still time!

Still too terrified to move? When the tip of the tail stiffens, you've gotten your final warning. The trick was to move away before that happened. Now you're in real trouble. So what's next? Bang-bang. You're it! You stink!

Armed with enough ammunition for four or five shots, able to shoot as far as 12 feet, the skunk lets loose with an oily, golden liquid that it keeps stored in two grape-sized sacs embedded in the muscle tissue on either side of its ANUS (ay-nuss).

A little tube extends from each of these sacs to the skunk's butt. Each ends in a nipple kind of like the ones you've got on your chest. But these are inside the skunk's butt. A SPHINCTER (sfink-ter) muscle holds the whole thing shut. When the skunk gets scared, it "moons" its enemy, and then relaxes the sphincter muscle while tightening the muscles around the sacs, and lets go!

Out comes a stream of that oily, noxious fluid ("noxious" means "really stinky") that's so strong it can make you sick to your stomach and cause temporary blindness if it gets in your eyes. And skunks, except for baby ones, have perfect aim. Fortunately for the next person who trips over the little fella, that skunk will not be able to "skunk" anyone else anytime soon. It takes between one and ten days to recharge. Does that make you feel any better?

Most animals figure out early on that any meeting with a skunk is basically a no-win situation. The biggest, meanest bear that comes face-to-face with a delicate little skunk will haul tail and get out of the way fast. Let's face it: A little cowardly behavior beats being temporarily blinded by a shot of skunk spray. The exception to this rule of animal behavior is the dog, who just never seems to get with the program. But what do you expect from something that drinks from the toilet bowl?

What if you get skunked? Take a bath in tomato juice, right? Wrong! That really doesn't work all that well. This strange custom started because skunk-stink is caused by a substance in the musk called MERCAPTAN (*mur-cap-tan*), a very strong BASE. A base is the chemical opposite of an acid. When you mix a *base* and an acid together, they sort of cancel each other out. Tomato juice has a lot of acid in it, so it seemed like it should cancel out the mercaptan, but it just doesn't work well enough. That's because the skunk's stinky stuff is also full of oil and sticks to everything it touches. So you have to break down the oily part, too.

Try this remedy instead: Fill a bathtub with warm water and a few squirts of dishwashing liquid. Add some water to half a cup of baking soda and mix it into a paste. Now toss the offending body (whether that's you, or your dog or cat) into the tub and rub the mixture all over. Follow with a vinegar rinse. Then rinse that off with soap and water. This works a whole lot better than tomato juice.

But guess what works best. A campfire! Wood smoke is a perfect natural antidote. Within minutes, the smoke will suck away all that skunky smell. The smoke works in two ways. A substance in smoke called CREOSOTE (*cree-oh-soht*) is very acidic, so it neutralizes the base. The smoke also seeps into any organic materials—like fabric, hair, or skin—it comes in contact with. (That's why your clothes always smell so, well, smoky when you've been hanging around a campfire.) Anyway, which would you rather smell like? A campfire or a skunk butt?

The Monkey's Paw

by W. W. Jacobs

If someone told you that you could have three wishes come true, you'd want that, wouldn't you? In this famous old story, you'll see how Mr. White is indeed granted three wishes. For many people—maybe you, too—getting three wishes would be a dream come true. Find out how Mr. White's dream turns into a nightmare.

utside, the night was cold and wet, but in the Whites' living room, a fire burned brightly. Father and son were playing chess. "Listen to the wind," said Mr. White. He'd made a bad move, and he was hoping his son Herbert wouldn't notice.

"I hear it," said Herbert, taking advantage of his father's mistake. "Check."

"I don't think that my old friend will make it here tonight," said Mr. White, making another move.

"Checkmate," replied his son, as he won the game.

"That's the worst part of living so far out," said Mr. White. "The road is always washed out."

"Never mind, dear," said his wife. "Perhaps you'll win the next game."

Just then, the gate banged loudly, and heavy footsteps came toward the door.

"Your friend made it after all," said Herbert.

The old man got up and opened the door. Then he led his friend into the living room.

"This is Major Morris," he said. "He was in the army. He's been everywhere and seen everything."

Morris shook hands and sat down by the fire. As he warmed up, his eyes got brighter. He began to talk. Everyone listened as he told stories about strange scenes, bloody wars, and horrible plagues.

"He's been gone 21 years," said Mr. White, nodding at his wife and son. "When he went away, he was a young man working with me in the warehouse. I'd like to travel, too, you know."

"You're better off where you are," said Morris, shaking his head. He put down the empty glass.

"I'd like to see old temples and mysterious objects," said the old man. "What were you telling me the other day? Something about a monkey's paw?"

"Oh, that was nothing. It's just something that they think is magic over in a faraway country," said Morris.

The White family leaned forward. Morris absentmindedly put his empty glass to his lips and then set it down again. Mr. White filled it for him.

"I think I've got the stupid thing here," said Morris, pulling something out of his pocket. "It looks just like an ordinary paw, all dried up."

Mrs. White drew back, but her son

took it and looked at it curiously.

"What's special about it?" asked Mr. White. He took it from his son and set it down on the table.

"An old man put a spell on it," said Morris. "He wanted to show that fate ruled people's lives, and that those who interfered would regret it. The spell grants three separate people three wishes."

"So are you going to give it a try?" asked Herbert.

"I have," Morris said quietly, and his face whitened.

"Did your wishes come true?" asked Mrs. White.

"They did," said Morris, and his glass tapped against his teeth.

"Has anybody else tried it?" asked Mrs. White.

"The first man had his three wishes. I don't know what the first two were, but the third was for death. That's how I got the paw."

His voice sounded so sad that the others grew quiet.

"If you've had your three wishes, then it's no good to you now," said Mr. White at last. "Why do you still have it?"

Morris shook his head. "I thought once that I would sell it, but I probably won't. It has caused enough trouble, and besides, people won't buy it. Some think it's a fairy tale. Others want to try it first and pay me later."

"If you could have another three wishes," asked Mr. White, "would you want them?"

Morris didn't answer. He just took the paw and threw it into the fire. Mr. White, with a little cry, bent and snatched it out of the flames.

"Better let it burn," said Morris.

"If you don't want it," said Mr. White, "why not give it to me?"

"No. I threw it on the fire. If you keep it, don't blame me for what happens. Throw it back, please."

The old man shook his head and stared at the paw. "How do you do it?"

"Hold it up in your right hand and wish aloud," said Morris, "but I'm telling you not to do it."

"It does sound like a fairy tale," said Mrs. White, as she got up and began to put the dinner on the table. "Why don't you wish for four pairs of hands for me?"

Mr. White held up the monkey's paw as Morris, looking alarmed, caught him by the arm. "If you must wish," he said, "wish for something sensible."

Mr. White dropped the paw into his pocket and led his friend to the table. As everyone ate, they all forgot about the paw. Then, after dinner, they sat listening as Morris told more stories about his adventures.

Finally, they closed the door behind their guest. "If the story about the monkey's paw isn't any more truthful than his other tall tales," said Mr. White, "there's not much to it."

"Did you give him anything for it?" asked his wife.

"Not much. He didn't want it, but I made him take it. He begged me again to throw the thing away."

"Wish to be king, Father," said Herbert. "Then nobody can boss you around."

Mr. White took the paw from his pocket and eyed it doubtfully. "I don't know what to wish for," he said. "I've really got all I want."

"If you paid off the mortgage on the house, you would be completely happy," said Herbert. "Wish for 2,000 dollars to do that."

Mr. White held up the paw. His son

sat down at the piano, and laughing, struck a few impressed chords.

"I wish for 2,000 dollars," said the old man. Then he let out a strange little cry and dropped the paw to the floor.

His wife and son ran toward him.

"It moved," he said. "As I wished, it twisted in my hands like a snake."

"Well, I don't see the 2,000 dollars," said his son, picking up the paw and putting it on the table. "And I bet I never do."

"That's impossible. You must have imagined it," said his wife, looking at him anxiously.

He shook his head. "No, I felt it move. I'm all right, but it gave me a shock just the same." Then he felt cold . . . and a little afraid.

The next morning, the sun streamed over the breakfast table, and Mr. White laughed at his fears. The room looked cheery, and the shriveled old paw lay on the counter, looking completely ordinary.

"I suppose all old soldiers are the same," said Mrs. White. "How could we have listened to that nonsense? How could three wishes be granted? If they could, how could getting the mortgage money hurt you?"

"The money might drop on his head from the sky," said Herbert.

"Morris said that everything happens so naturally," said his father, "that you might think it was all just a big coincidence."

"Well, don't spend all the money before I come back," said Herbert, rising from the table. "I'm afraid it'll turn you into a greedy old man."

"Herbert will make more funny remarks when he comes home from work," Mrs. White said after her son had been gone awhile.

"I wouldn't be surprised," said Mr.

White, "but the thing really did move in my hand. I'd swear to that."

"At least, you *thought* it moved."

"It did," he said. Then he looked up at his wife, who staring out the window. "What's the matter?"

She didn't answer. She was watching a man, who seemed to be trying to decide whether to knock on their door. She noticed that he was well dressed and wearing an expensive suit. Three times he walked past their gate, then turned and walked back. The fourth time, he opened the gate and walked up the path. Mrs. White got up and opened the door.

She brought the man into the house and waited for him to say something. At first, he was silent. "I was asked to come here," he said at last, stopping to pick lint off his pants. "I'm from Maw and Meggins."

Mrs. White was startled. "Is anything the matter?" she asked anxiously. "Has anything happened to Herbert at work?"

Her husband interrupted. "There, there," he said. "Don't jump to conclusions. You're not bringing us bad news, are you?" he asked the man.

"I'm sorry..."

"Is he hurt?" demanded Mrs. White.

The man nodded. "Badly hurt," he said quietly, "but he is not in any pain."

"Oh, thank heavens!" said the old woman. "Thank heavens for that! Thank –"

She broke off suddenly as she realized what the man really meant. Herbert was dead. She caught her breath, and turning to her husband, put her trembling hand on his. There was a long silence.

"I'm afraid that he was caught in the machinery this morning," said the man finally.

"Caught in the machinery," repeated Mr. White.

He sat, staring blankly out the

window, and pressed his wife's hand between his own.

"He was the only son we had," he said, turning to the visitor. "It is hard."

The man coughed and walked slowly to the window. "The firm wanted me to give you their sincere sympathy," he said, not looking around. "Please understand that I am only an employee, and I'm only obeying orders."

Neither Mr. nor Mrs. White replied. Their faces were white, their eyes staring.

"They told me to say that Maw and Meggins is not responsible for what happened. Still, they want to present you with a certain sum of money."

Mr. White gazed with horror at the visitor. His dry lips shaped the words, "How much?"

"Two thousand dollars."

Mr. White didn't even hear his wife's scream. He smiled faintly, put out his hands like a blind man, and fell to the floor.

The Whites buried their son in a huge new cemetery two miles away. They came back to a house filled with shadows and silence. It was all over so quickly that at first they could hardly believe it. They kept waiting for something else to happen, something to make their lives easier to bear.

About a week after the funeral, Mr. White woke up in the middle of the night. He stretched out his hand and found himself alone in the darkness. He heard his wife weeping by the window. "Come back," he said tenderly. "You will be cold."

"It is colder for my son," she said and kept crying.

He went back to sleep until a sudden wild cry from his wife woke him with a start. "The monkey's paw!" she cried wildly. "The monkey's paw!"

He looked up in alarm. "Where is it? What's happened? What's the matter?"

She stumbled across the room toward him. "I want it," she said. "You haven't destroyed it, have you?"

"It's in the living room. Why?"

She bent over and kissed his cheek. "Why didn't I think of it before? Why didn't you think of it?"

"Think of what?"

"The other two wishes. We've only had one."

"Wasn't that enough?"

"No," she said. "We'll have one more. Go down and get the monkey's paw, and wish our son alive again."

The man sat up in bed and threw off the covers. "You're crazy!"

"We had the first wish granted," said Mrs. White. "Why not the second?"

"A coincidence," he stammered.

"Go and get it!"

Mr. White's voice shook. "I don't think you want him back. He has been dead 10 days. When he was killed, he was so mangled that I could only recognize him by his clothing."

"Bring him back," she demanded. "Do you think I'm afraid of my own child?"

He went down in the darkness, and felt his way to the living room. He found the monkey's paw on the mantel. Then he felt his way along the wall until he found himself in the hall.

Even his wife's face seemed different as he entered the room. He was almost afraid of her. "Wish!" she cried, in a strong voice.

"It is foolish and wrong," he protested.

"Wish!" she repeated.

He raised his hand. "I wish my son alive again."

The monkey's paw jerked in his hand and fell to the floor. He sank into a chair as his wife walked to the window and opened the blinds.

He sat until he was chilled with the cold. He glanced now and then at his wife peering through the window. The candle threw shadows on the ceiling and walls until, finally, it flickered out. Nothing happened. Their son did not come back. Mr. White crawled back to bed with a sense of relief. A minute or two later, his wife lay down silently beside him.

Neither spoke, but both lay listening to the ticking of the clock. A stair creaked, and squeaky mouse scurried through the wall. The darkness bothered the old man. Finally, he took the box of matches and, striking one, he went downstairs for a candle.

At the foot of the stairs, the match went out. He stopped to strike another. At that moment, he heard a knock on the front door.

The matches fell from his hand. He stood motionless, not breathing until he heard the knock again. Then he turned, ran back to his room, and closed the door behind him. A third knock sounded through the house.

"What's that?" cried Mrs. White.

"A rat," said Mr. White, shaking. "A rat passed me on the stairs."

His wife sat up in bed, listening. The knocking started again.

"It's Herbert!" she screamed. "It's Herbert!"

She ran to the door, but her husband got there before her. He caught her by the arm in the hallway and held her tightly.

"What are you going to do?" he whispered.

"It's my boy. It's Herbert!" she cried. "I forgot the cemetery was two miles away. That's what took so long! Why are you holding me back? Let go. I have to open the door."

"Don't let it in," cried Mr. White, trembling.

"You're afraid of your own son. Let me go. I'm coming, Herbert!"

There was another knock and another. Mrs. White pulled free and ran from the room. Her husband had reached the landing when he heard her voice, strained and panting.

"The door bolt! Come help me. It's too high for me to reach."

But her husband was on his hands and knees. He was reaching wildly for the paw. If he could only find it before the thing outside got in. He heard a chair scrape as his wife put it down in front of the door. He heard the creaking of the door bolt as she pushed it back. At the same moment, he found the monkey's paw. He frantically made his third and last wish.

The knocking stopped suddenly, although its echoes were still in the house. He heard the door open, and a cold wind rushed up the stairs. His wife's long, loud wail of misery gave him the courage to run to her side. He looked out the door and past the gate. The street lamp shone on a quiet and deserted road.

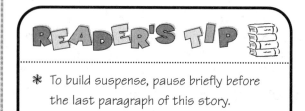

* To build suspense, pause briefly before the last paragraph of this story.

Eleven

by Sandra Cisneros

Have you ever heard someone say to you, "Act your age!"? What, exactly, does that saying mean? Do you think it's possible for someone who is 10, or 12, or 13 to act lots of different ages? Can they act all grown up one minute and not so grown up the next? Listen to this story about a girl who has just turned 11. Ask yourself, "What is she feeling? And, Why?"

What they don't understand about birthdays and what they never tell you is that when you're eleven, you're also ten, and nine, and eight, and seven, and six, and five, and four, and three, and two, and one. And when you wake up on your eleventh birthday you expect to feel eleven, but you don't. You open your eyes and everything's just like yesterday, only it's today. And you don't feel eleven at all. You feel like you're still ten. And you are—underneath the year that makes you eleven.

Like some days you might say something stupid, and that's the part of you that's still ten. Or maybe some days you might need to sit on your mama's lap because you're scared, and that's the part of you that's five. And maybe one day when you're all grown up maybe you will need to cry like if you're three, and that's okay. That's what I tell Mama when she's sad and needs to cry. Maybe she's feeling three.

Because the way you grow old is kind of like an onion or like the rings inside a tree trunk or like my little wooden dolls that fit one inside the other, each year inside the next one. That's how being eleven years old is.

You don't feel eleven. Not right away. It takes a few days, weeks even, sometimes even months before you say Eleven when they ask you. And you don't feel smart eleven, not until you're almost twelve. That's the way it is.

Only today I wish I didn't have only eleven years rattling inside me like pennies in a tin Band-Aid box. Today I wish I was one hundred and two instead of eleven because if I was one hundred and two I'd have known what to say when Mrs. Price put the red sweater on my desk. I would've known how to tell her it wasn't mine instead of just sitting there with that look on my face and nothing coming out of my mouth.

"Whose is this?" Mrs. Price says, and she holds the red sweater up in the air for all the class to see. "Whose? It's been sitting in the coatroom for a month."

"Not mine," says everybody. "Not me."

"It has to belong to somebody," Mrs. Price keeps saying, but nobody can remember. It's an ugly sweater with red plastic buttons and a collar and sleeves all stretched out like you could use it for a jump rope. It's maybe a thousand years old and even if it belonged to me I wouldn't say so.

Maybe because I'm skinny, maybe because she doesn't like me, that stupid Sylvia Saldívar says, "I think it belongs to Rachel." An ugly sweater like that, all raggedy and old, but Mrs. Price believes her. Mrs. Price takes the sweater and puts it right on my desk, but when I open my mouth nothing comes out.

"That's not, I don't, you're not . . . Not mine," I finally say in a little voice that was maybe me when I was four.

"Of course it's yours," Mrs. Price says. "I remember you wearing it once." Because she's older and the teacher, she's right and I'm not.

Not mine, not mine, not mine, but Mrs. Price is already turning to page thirty-two, and math problem number four. I don't know why but all of a sudden I'm feeling sick inside, like the part of me that's three wants to come out of my eyes, only I squeeze them shut tight and bite down on my teeth real hard and try to remember today I am eleven, eleven. Mama is making a cake for me for tonight, and when Papa comes home everybody will sing Happy birthday, happy birthday to you.

But when the sick feeling goes away and I open my eyes, the red sweater's still sitting there like a big red mountain. I move the red sweater to the corner of my desk with my ruler. I move my pencil and books and eraser as far from it as possible. I even move my chair a little to the right. Not mine, not mine, not mine.

In my head I'm thinking how long till lunchtime, how long till I can take the red sweater and throw it over the schoolyard fence, or leave it hanging on a parking meter, or bunch it up into a little ball and toss it in the alley. Except when math period ends Mrs. Price says loud and in front of everybody, "Now, Rachel, that's enough," because she sees I've shoved the red sweater to the tippy-tip corner of my desk and it 's hanging all over the edge like a waterfall, but I don't care.

"Rachel," Mrs. Price says. She says it like she's getting mad. "You put that sweater on right now and no more nonsense."

"But it's not—"

"Now!" Mrs. Price says.

This is when I wish I wasn't eleven, because all the years inside of me—ten, nine, eight, seven, six, five, four, three, two and one—are pushing at the back of my eyes when I put one arm through one sleeve of the sweater that smells like cottage cheese, and then the other arm through the other and stand there with my arms apart like if the sweater hurts me and it does, all itchy and full of germs that aren't even mine.

That's when everything I've been holding in since this morning, since when Mrs. Price put the sweater on my desk, finally lets go, and all of a sudden I'm crying in front of everybody. I wish I was invisible but I'm not. I'm eleven and it's my birthday today and I'm crying like I'm three in front of everybody. I put my head down on the desk and bury my face in my stupid clown-sweater arms. My face all hot and spit coming out of my mouth because I can't stop the little animal noises from coming out of me, until there aren't any more tears left in my eyes, and it's just my body shaking like when you have the hiccups, and my whole head hurts like when you drink milk too fast.

But the worst part is right before the bell rings for lunch. That stupid Phyllis Lopez, who is even dumber than Sylvia Saldívar, says she remembers the red sweater is hers! I take it off right away and give it to her, only Mrs. Price pretends like everything's okay.

Today I'm eleven. There's a cake Mama's making for tonight, and when Papa comes home from work we'll eat it. There'll be candles and presents and everybody will sing Happy birthday, happy birthday to you, Rachel, only it's too late.

I'm eleven today. I'm eleven, ten, nine, eight, seven, six, five, four, three, two and one, but I wish I was one hundred and two. I wish I was anything but eleven, because I want today to be far away already, far away like a runaway balloon, like a tiny dot in the sky, so tiny-tiny you have to close your eyes to see it.

Whale Hunters

by Alexandra Hanson-Harding

Can you think of a few dangerous jobs? Why do you think people choose to do risky and dangerous work? This story I'm about to tell takes place hundreds of years ago, back when adventurous men often risked their lives hunting whales! The whalers needed danger to stay happy. For them, a life without danger was too boring.

Reuben Delano, a sailor in the 1840s, once wrote, "On the seventh day from our departure from the Japan coast at 2:00 P.M., a whale was seen from the masthead, and the cheering cry of 'there she blows' resounded through the ship." Whaling crews were always waiting and hoping to hear "there she blows!" To them, this phrase meant possible riches and an end to the boredom.

Whaling was big business in the 1800s. Whale oil provided fuel for lamps. The bones and cartilage were used in products such as women's corsets. Spermaceti, from the whale's head, was used in candle-making. But the most valuable of all was ambergris, a waxy substance from the intestines that was used in expensive perfumes.

✳

Native Americans first taught the white settlers how to catch whales. Whale hunting became an important business for colonists in places like Sag Harbor, New York, and Nantucket Island,

Massachusetts. At first, whaling ships stayed close to shore. But in 1712, sea captain Christopher Hussey's ship was blown out to sea in a huge storm. The crew found themselves surrounded by sperm whales. Hussey and his crew caught one and brought it back to Nantucket. Soon, other whaling ships also sailed out to catch the larger whales.

Before long, ships carried try-pots on board. These were large pots for boiling whale blubber into oil. With the try-pots, the whalers no longer needed to return to shore. Soon, American whaling ships were sailing all over the world.

Here's how the whalers actually killed the whales. When they spotted one, they lowered small boats into the water. Then they rowed as close to the whale as they could. One sailor would hurl a heavy harpoon (barbed spear) at it. The wounded whale would then struggle to get free. The more the whale struggled, the more the harpoon would tear its blubber. The maddened whale would usually swim away from the boat, dragging the crew behind it on what came to be called a "Nantucket sleigh ride." The whalers would hold on tight for hours until the whale had lost too much blood to keep swimming. When the whale slowed down, the crew would row even closer to the whale and shove a lance into its side. And that would be the end of the whale.

Catching a whale was risky work. A sailor named Henry Cheever wrote, "Sometimes the mammoth brute comes up from the depths right under the boat, and takes it, with all on board into his huge mouth, that can be opened 16 and 20 feet. To be sure, the monster does not swallow [the boat], but he crushes it to pieces as if it were an eggshell, and, not infrequently, some of its crew at the same time."

The crew would tow the whale back to the main ship and chain it to the side of the ship. Then they would slice up the whale's sides, cut the blubber (fat) into smaller pieces, and toss it into try-pots to boil into oil.

The oil was poured into huge casks and stored. This dangerous, filthy work, done on a slippery deck in rolling seas, could take three or four days.

Sailor Henry Bullen said that the most dangerous part of the job was filling and shifting the giant casks of oil. "Some of these were of enormous size," he noted, "containing 350 gallons when full, and the work of moving them about the greasy deck of a rolling ship was attended with a terrible amount of risk."

Many first-time sailors on whaling ships expected wonderful adventures on tropical islands. But sailing life was dirty and dangerous. The ships were filthy and smelly. The food was disgusting. A typical dish was lobscouse—a stew of rancid pork fat, crumbled hardtack (hard, dry

biscuit), and molasses.

Sailors slept on hard bunks or in hammocks in a dark, cramped cabin. They shared their cabins with rats and roaches. The work was hard and the pay was poor. Still, many enjoyed the excitement of whaling. Henry Cheever wrote, "I like the eagerness and activity and can very well put up with the smell and dirt which having dead whales alongside makes in a whale ship."

Sailors faced storms, disease, and other dangers. The most notorious journey was the South Sea adventure of the whaleship *Essex*. On November 19, 1819, the ship was sailing along when a sperm whale suddenly rammed it. "The ship was brought up as suddenly and violently as if she had struck a rock, and trembled for a few seconds like a leaf," wrote Owen Chase, first mate of the *Essex*. "We looked at each other with perfect amazement, deprived almost of the power of speech." The ship soon sank. "All that remained," said Chase, "to conduct these 20 beings through the stormy terrors of the ocean, perhaps many thousand miles, were three open light boats."

The crew of the *Essex* drifted 2,500 miles for two-and-a-half months before they were spotted. By that time, only five men were left—and they had survived by cannibalizing (eating) the others.

In the 1850s, the new petroleum industry became more important than whaling. Also, the whalers were running out of whales. The waters where the whalers hunted were nearly empty. By the end of the 1920s, the whaling industry in the U.S. had pretty much died out.

Whaling left an important legacy, however. It had helped to populate the coastal areas of the Northeast and develop the country financially.

The whalers also made important discoveries. They were the first to notice the Gulf Stream. And they mapped much of the South Pacific Ocean and other parts of the world, helping trade to grow and flourish.

As Herman Melville wrote in *Moby Dick*, a novel published in 1851, "I freely assert that the [city dweller] cannot, for his life, point out one single peaceful influence, which within the last 60 years has operated more potentially upon the whole broad world . . . than the high and mighty business of whaling."

The U.S. and most other Western countries no longer allow whale hunting. But a few countries, including Japan and Norway, still permit it. Some native peoples are allowed to hunt because eating whale meat is a cultural tradition.

The International Whaling Commission (IWC) imposed a moratorium (ban) on whaling in 1986. Whale hunting is only allowed for science. Japan kills about 500 minke whales a year. Japanese scientists test the animals and insist that the hunt meets IWC standards. But the meat winds up on Japanese tables in the end.

Cutting back on whale hunting has allowed many whale populations to recover. According to the IWC, there are between 500,000 and 1 million minke whales alive today. But some whale species remain endangered, such as the blue whale—the world's largest. There are only about 3,500 blue whales left.

Bandaids and Five Dollar Bills

by Sharon M. Draper

The poem you are about to hear is told from a teacher's point of view. In it, the teacher asks her students, "How would you change the world?" Listen for how one boy's simple request comes about because of his not-so-simple life.

My students wrote essays for homework this week,
The usual stuff for grade ten,
I asked them to write how they'd change the world
If the changing was left up to them.

His name was Rick Johnson; he was surly and shy,
A student who's always ignored.
He'd slouch in his seat with a Malcolm X cap,
Half-sleep, making sure he looked bored.

His essay was late—just before I went home,
It was wrinkled and scribbled and thin,
I thought to reject it . . . (Why do teachers do that?)
But I thanked him for turning it in.

"You can't cure the world," his essay began,
"Of the millions of evils and ills,
But to clean up my world so I could survive,
I'd cut bandaids and five dollar bills.

"Now bandaids are beige—says right on the box
'Skin tone' is the color inside.
Whose skin tone? Not mine! Been lookin' for years
For someone with that color hide.

"Cause bandaids show up, looking pasty and pale,
It's hard to pretend they're not there,
When the old man has beat me and I gotta get stitches,
Them bandaids don't cover or care.

"And now, you may ask, why would anyone want
To get rid of five dollar bills?
Cause for just that much cash, a dude's mama can buy
A crack rock, or whiskey, or pills.

"She smokes it or drinks it, and screams at her kids,
Then passes out cold on the floor,
By morn she remembers no pain, just the void,
And her kids wish the world had a door.

"So my magical dream not out of reach,
Like curing cancer or AIDS, or huge ills,
All I ask from my life is a little respect,
And no bandaids or five dollar bills."

Sick

by Shel Silverstein

How many of you have ever wanted to miss a day of school? How many of you have wanted to miss a day of school so badly that you were willing to stretch the truth a bit? You're about to hear a poem where the truth is being stretched. Really stretched!

"I cannot go to school today,"
Said little Peggy Ann McKay.
"I have the measles and the mumps,
A gash, a rash and purple bumps.
My mouth is wet, my throat is dry,
I'm going blind in my right eye.
My tonsils are as big as rocks,
I've counted sixteen chicken pox
And there's one more—that's seventeen,
And don't you think my face looks green?
My leg is cut, my eyes are blue—
It might be instamatic flu.
I cough and sneeze and gasp and choke,
I'm sure that my left leg is broke—
My hip hurts when I move my chin,
My belly button's caving in,
My back is wrenched, my ankle's sprained,
My 'pendix pains each time it rains.
My nose is cold, my toes are numb,
I have a sliver in my thumb.
My neck is stiff, my voice is weak,
I hardly whisper when I speak.
My tongue is filling up my mouth,
I think my hair is falling out.
My elbow's bent, my spine ain't straight,
My temperature is one-o-eight.
My brain is shrunk, I cannot hear,
There is a hole inside my ear.
I have a hangnail, and my heart is—what?
What's that? What's that you say?
You say today is . . . Saturday?
G'bye, I'm going out to play!"

READER'S TIP

* Varying the speed in which you read the lines of this poem will add to its humor and enjoyment.

9/11—An Eyewitness Account

by Suzanne McCabe

Suzanne McCabe is a writer and an editor for *Junior Scholastic Magazine* in New York City. In the early morning of 9/11/01, Suzanne was on a ferry headed to work. It was during her commute that the attack on the World Trade Center occurred. In this eyewitness account of the 9/11 tragedy, you'll see why this horrible event was even more painful for her.

"As you can see," the ferry captain said over his bullhorn, "a plane has crashed into the World Trade Center."

It was 8:48, and our commuter boat had just left Atlantic Highlands, New Jersey, for New York City. It was the kind of morning pilots call "severe clear." We could see the skyscrapers of lower Manhattan—still 40 minutes away—with aching clarity.

Like everyone else, I watched in horror as smoke spewed from the upper floors of the north tower. Metal strips that had encased the building began to unfurl like cans of tuna fish.

Then it dawned on me: My brother Michael was somewhere inside that 110-story building.

A week earlier, Mike had joined one of his best friends, Mike Tucker, or "Tuck," at Cantor Fitzgerald, an international brokerage firm. Before that, Mike had worked at Prudential Bache for 18 years.

Mike and Tuck traded over-the-counter stocks and rode the same boat each morning. They were always at their desks by 7:30.

I knew they would be in their office, I just didn't know what floor it was on. I tried to reach Mike—then his wife, Lynn, then my brother Nick. No answer anywhere.

Just as I looked up, a second plane sliced through the upper floors of the south tower. Everyone gasped. That ruthless smack knocked the wind out of all of us. This was no accident. America, we realized, was under attack.

Still, we sailed on. We passed the Sandy Hook Lighthouse, the Statue of Liberty, and Ellis Island, all eyes on those twin towers. Black smoke billowed from one. Orange and yellow fireballs, the size of zeppelins, ringed the other.

We watched in disbelief as shards of glass and paper rained down on the streets below. I tried to imagine Mike and Tuck running down the stairs to safety.

✳

As we approached New York Harbor, the captain announced that no one could disembark. Instead, we would pick up those who had fled office buildings near the trade center.

Black soot and ash now cloaked much of the sky. The smell of burning plastic and rubber soured the air.

Already, thousands of people had crammed the pier. Knowing better, I looked for Mike's face in the crowd.

As we headed back to Atlantic Highlands, I went up to the top deck. Lower Manhattan looked ghastly. But nothing could prepare me for what came next: the collapse of the south tower. Within seconds it seemed, a huge swirl of ash and debris took down the once soaring skyscraper, changing a landscape I had known and loved since childhood.

A friend held me as a group of us watched in silence. Almost no one could get through to family and friends.

Somewhere, though, a cell phone rang. "It's my sister," a woman said. "The Pentagon's been hit!" Faces froze in disbelief. So this is war, I thought.

After the north tower fell, I estimated how much time Mike and Tuck would have needed to escape. I knew that many of the firefighters, whose trucks we heard screaming down Broadway, would be crushed by falling debris.

✳

My brother Michael did not make it home on September 11. Within 48 hours, his body was pulled from a mound of twisted steel, metal, and concrete. He and Tuck had been on the 104th floor of the north tower, too high up to be saved.

The world lost two great guys on September 11. They were loving husbands and fathers, brothers and sons, and two of the most talented traders on Wall Street. My brother Mike was a loyal friend and superb basketball player.

In the span of an hour or so, maybe less, the world lost thousands of other greats. Many were traders, like Mike and Tuck. Others were firefighters, police officers, and chaplains. Still others were violinists, chefs, and photographers— scholars, skiers, thinkers, and dreamers.

When the terrorists sliced off the top floors of the twin towers, they took some of the best and brightest. They left thousands of children without a dad or a mom. They broke our hearts but not our spirits.

The Attack on Pearl Harbor

by Sean Price

Perhaps you can remember very clearly where you were on the morning of 9/11/01. Certainly your parents remember that horrible day. There is another day, however, that many older Americans remember. December 7th, 1941, was the day of another attack on America.

n the morning of December 7, 1941, Stephen Bower Young, a 19-year-old sailor on the USS *Oklahoma*, was a happy man. It was a beautiful Sunday morning at Pearl Harbor, Hawaii, and he had plans to go on a picnic with his girlfriend.

Then, just before 8 A.M., two bugle blasts sounded over the battleship's loudspeaker. Young later remembered how puzzled he and his crewmates were: "A voice boomed throughout the ship,: 'All hands on deck, man your battle stations!' What the heck was this? Drills on Sunday? They knew we were all waiting to go ashore. The harsh, excited voice on the PA system froze us in our tracks. 'All hands on deck, man your battle stations! On the double! This is no drill! Get going—they're real bombs!'"

That day, Japanese warplanes swooped down and bombed most of the U.S. battleships based in the Pacific Ocean, along with 188 planes. The attack left 2,400 people dead and 1,200 wounded.

Until September 11, 2001, Pearl Harbor was the most horrible attack the U.S. had ever suffered on its own soil. Like the terrorist attacks on New York and Washington, D.C., it was a historic turning point. Pearl Harbor shocked Americans and pushed the U.S. into World War II.

✳

You're probably wondering why Japan bombed Pearl Harbor. Well, the attack had its roots in the Great Depression—a worldwide economic downturn that lasted from 1929 to 1940. The Depression hit Germany and Japan hard. Poverty and unrest in both countries caused democratic governments to fall. They were replaced by dictatorships bent on conquering the world.

Starting in 1931, military leaders gradually took control of Japan's government. They began a long, bloody invasion in China with an eye toward controlling the entire Far East.

In 1933, Adolf Hitler and his Nazi Party seized control of Germany. Germany attacked Poland in September 1939, starting World War II in Europe. A year later, Germany, Japan, and Italy—another dictatorship—formed the Axis alliance.

At that time, many Americans were isolationists—they were opposed to U.S. involvement in foreign affairs. They cared more about ending unemployment at home than fighting overseas. By early 1941, however, Hitler had gobbled up most of Europe. Japan was poised to conquer Asia.

U.S. President Franklin D. Roosevelt tried to convince the American people that war was necessary. But the Americans didn't want it. Nor did they want a military draft—which would mean that all young men once they turned 18 would be required to serve in the armed forces. They also didn't want tax money spent on building new planes and ships.

But that all changed. Here's what happened.

✳

Japanese officials were getting ready. They could not resist attacking Pearl Harbor. They believed that with one lightning strike, they could crush their strongest foe—the U.S. Navy.

U.S. leaders had warnings that an attack was coming. In fact, they had broken one of Japan's secret codes. But the hints and signs of danger were like pieces of a puzzle that nobody put together.

Warnings even came on the morning of the attack. An alert from Washington calling for greater watchfulness at Pearl Harbor was misrouted by a telegraph operator. A U.S. destroyer caught and sank a strange-looking submarine just outside the harbor. Radar operators spotted planes coming toward Hawaii but mistook them for U.S. bombers.

How could all these warnings have been ignored? Americans underestimated the Japanese. Japan was on the other side of the Pacific Ocean, 3,000 miles away. Few Americans thought Japan had the skill or the weapons to attack Pearl Harbor.

But they did, and 6-year-old Dorinda Nicholson had a ringside seat for the attack. Her family was eating breakfast in their home near Pearl Harbor when suddenly warplanes roared overhead.

"We shielded our eyes from the early morning sun," said Nicholson, "and looked up into the orange-red emblem of the Rising Sun [Japan's wartime flag]. The planes were so low, just barely above the rooftops, that we could see the pilots' faces and even the goggles that covered their eyes."

The Japanese destroyed most of the U.S. planes on the ground. Then they sent bombs screaming into eight U.S. battleships and dozens of smaller vessels (ships). On some ships, the ammunition for anti-aircraft guns was locked up tight. Frustrated sailors threw wrenches and fired rifles at the low-flying planes.

Within minutes, thousands of men were dead or wounded.

In situations like this, people do things they wouldn't normally do. For instance, on the battleship USS *California*, sailor John McGoran tried to rescue an injured man he had never liked. "If on December 6th anyone had asked me to help save the life of this offensive guy, I would have answered, 'To heck with him,'" said McGoran. "I had known this fellow since boot camp, and he was one of the most obnoxious individuals I had ever met. But now . . . his was a life to be saved."

✳

Because of the time difference between Hawaii and the U.S. mainland, most Americans did not hear about Pearl Harbor until Sunday afternoon. Shock and disbelief quickly gave way to anger and fear. Some panicked. In Florence, Alabama, 13-year-old Douglas Jaynes ran through the streets yelling, "The Japs have bombed Pearl Harbor, and they're headed for us on Four Mile Creek."

Many Americans were mistakenly paranoid like Jaynes. In the days that followed the attack, rumors convinced thousands that a Japanese invasion force was about to land in California. Air-raid sirens—each one a false alarm—wailed all over the U.S. In Los Angeles, anti-aircraft guns opened fire on planes that weren't there.

The Japanese were jubilant (overjoyed). They had crippled U.S. sea power and lost only 29 airplanes and 55 men. But the attack was not a complete success. Most of all, Japan had wanted to destroy U.S. aircraft carriers. But those ships had sailed from Pearl Harbor just days before.

The strike on Pearl Harbor left Americans united and thirsting for revenge. On December 8, President Roosevelt asked Congress to declare war. He called the previous day "a date which will live in infamy."

Back at Pearl Harbor, Stephen Bower Young was still on the *Oklahoma*. The great ship had capsized within 15 minutes of the first bombs falling. Young and hundreds of other men were trapped below decks. Rescue crews managed to save Young and 31 others. But 429 sailors couldn't be reached.

"Standing on the upturned hull, I gazed about me," said Young. "It was the same world I had left 25 hours before, but as I looked at the smoke and wreckage of battle . . . I felt that life would never be the same, not for me—not for any of us."

Only a Dollar's Worth

by Herma Werner

Some people believe that you should always treat people the way that they treat you. Certainly that makes sense if people treat you kindly and with respect. But what happens when someone treats you poorly? Should you treat them the same way? In the story you are about to hear, Isabel discovers that answering that question isn't as easy as it may sound.

I t was Mr. Watts again.

Isabel sighed and grabbed the hose. She took the cap from the gas tank and called through the car window, "A whole dollar's worth again, Mr. Watts?" She knew she sounded nasty, but she didn't care.

Mr. Watts got out of his old car. "Watch your smart mouth, little girl," he said. "You ought to know by now what I want. Maybe you ought to get a job a girl can do right."

Isabel knew the whole routine from start to finish, including the insults. Mr. Watts watched like a hawk as she ran a dollar's worth of gas into the tank. He didn't take his eyes off her. He watched to make sure that every drop of gas he paid for got into the tank.

Then the old man opened a beat-up wallet and fished out a dollar bill. He held on to the money as if it were a fortune in diamonds.

"Get that windshield clean," he said. "And the rear glass, too. How come I have to remind you every time? The boy that was here before never forgot."

Isabel looked at Mr. Watts with scorn. Every couple of days, he came around for a dollar's worth of gas. For a dollar, he felt he was entitled to a windshield cleaning—front, rear, and sides. His dollar's worth included water in the radiator once a week. And water for the battery once a month.

Every two weeks, Isabel gave the old car an oil check. But if the car needed oil, Mr. Watts would order it from an auto-supply store. Then he'd have his grandson add it for him. Cheap!, Isabel thought to herself. She wished the old man could read her mind.

She finished polishing the glass. "OK, Mr. Watts? That the way you want it?" she asked.

Mr. Watts shrugged and gave Isabel the money. "Do I have a choice?" he muttered. He climbed back in his car and drove off at about ten miles per hour.

Isabel turned and saw that her boss, Mr. Kirkland, had been watching. She handed him the dollar bill.

"Mr. Watts just paid off your mortgage," Isabel said sarcastically. Mr. Kirkland laughed, but Isabel just looked disgusted. "Why do you put up with him, Mr. Kirkland?" she asked.

"Oh, he's been doing that for years," Mr. Kirkland said. "He's old. He has nothing else to do all day. Let him have his fun."

"I wish he'd have his fun with somebody else," Isabel said. She had been working at Kirkland's Gas Station for a few months. She liked the job, but she had come to dread the sight of Mr. Watts. "I know he's not broke," she went on. "I heard he has a lot of money."

"Not true," said Mr. Kirkland. "Mr. Watts has a small pension. If he didn't live with his daughters, I don't know what he'd do." He turned to go back to the office. "Don't let it get to you, Isabel," he added. "It's just one of those things. There's nothing we can do."

"No?" Isabel thought to herself. "Just once I'd like to tell that old cheapskate what I think of him. I bet we wouldn't see him again after that."

She went back to the pumps. And there, right where the old man had stood, Isabel saw it. It was green and beautiful. It was a $20 bill. She scooped it up and stared at it for a while to make sure it was real. She figured that it had to belong to Mr. Watts.

She looked down the street. Mr. Watts would be coming back for it any minute. Quickly, she stuffed the bill into the pocket of her jeans.

Half an hour passed. Mr. Watts did not return. After an hour, Isabel felt that the $20 was really hers. She began to make all kinds of plans for it. She could see herself adding it to the money she'd saved for a car. After an hour and a half, she had switched to buying a new jacket. After two hours, she watched herself listening to the new tapes she wanted. Just then, Mr. Watts came driving into the station.

Isabel slipped a hand into her pocket and touched the bill. There was no way Mr. Watts could know she had it. After all, he could have lost it anyplace. She thought of all his insults—about girls working at gas stations, about how dumb she was. Maybe he deserved to pay for the way he treated her.

The old car sputtered to a halt in front of the gas pumps. Isabel stood with the hose in her hand. For the first time she really noticed the torn upholstery inside the car. She got a look at the old empty crate that always sat in the backseat.

Mr. Watts got out of the car. He seemed even slower than usual, and he stared down at the ground for what seemed a long time. Then he looked hard at Isabel.

"Listen here, Missy. That wasn't a dollar bill I gave you before. It was a 20."

Isabel felt her face grow hot. Why was he always so quick to blame her and put her down? He must know he gave her a dollar. So why lie about it? All of Isabel's doubts dissolved. Now she knew she had a right to the $20, but she was afraid he might make her empty her pockets.

"You give me the same thing every time you're here, Mr. Watts," she said. She met his eyes and stared him down. She was telling the truth, and he knew it.

"Today was different," said Mr. Watts. "You forgot to give me change, Miss Know-It-All. I want my money."

"You gave me a dollar bill," Isabel insisted. "That's the truth."

Mr. Kirkland came over to them, wiping his hands on a rag. "What's the trouble?" he asked.

"When I was here before I gave this . . .

. this girl of yours a $20 bill. She didn't give me any change," Mr. Watts said.

"No," Mr. Kirkland said. "Isabel handed me the money right after you left. It was a dollar bill. You're wrong, Mr. Watts. I hope you're not calling *me* a liar?"

Mr. Watts stared at Mr. Kirkland. Then he shook his head sadly and seemed to fold up into a tiny gray package right before Isabel's eyes. She tried to blink away the image, but it stayed.

She had never thought of Mr. Watts as anything but mean and cheap and nasty. But suddenly, she understood him better. She was young and strong and able to do what he considered a man's work. He was old and poor. He didn't like buying a dollar's worth of gas at a time. He had to be frugal. But he still had pride, so he covered up what he had to do with a lot of noise.

Isabel went over to the old car. She opened the door and looked into the back where the crate was.

"Hey, you, get out of there!" Mr. Watts called. It was the old nasty voice, but Isabel heard something else under the sharp words. Fear.

She stood up and turned. The $20 bill was in her hand. "Is this what you're looking for?" she said. She walked over to the two men.

Mr. Watts grabbed the bill and waved it under Mr. Kirkland's nose. His voice was loud and mean again.

"See?" Mr. Watts said. "I don't go around saying things that aren't true."

Without even a thank you, he climbed into his car and drove away. Mr. Kirkland gave Isabel a long, thoughtful look.

Isabel felt her face growing hot again, but she returned the look. After all, her only crime had been to dream a little.

"Think he'll be back?" she asked after a while.

"He'll be back," Mr. Kirkland said.

"For a dollar's worth?"

"I'm afraid so," laughed Mr. Kirkland. And this time, Isabel laughed too.

The Coal Mine Disaster

by Michael Dahlie

Which of the following are you really afraid of? Are you afraid of being buried alive? How about drowning? Or freezing to death? In late July 2002, nine coal miners in western Pennsylvania had to face these fears head on in one of the worst mining disasters in American history. What happened to them? Here's their story.

It was just another day at work for nine miners at the Quecreek coal mine in western Pennsylvania. They were hundreds of feet below ground doing what they had spent their lives doing—looking for coal. They were used to the dark, cold surroundings. They weren't afraid of being far beneath thousands of tons of solid rock. For them, the mine was no different from any other place of work.

The miners were exploring a new branch of the mine. According to their map, there was an abandoned mine about 100 yards away from them. Between their mine and the abandoned mine lay 300 feet of unexplored rock—a perfect place to look for coal.

But mining can be tricky business. The other mine had been abandoned decades earlier, and no one really knew too much about it. That was a problem. The maps the miners were using weren't as good as they had thought. When they started digging, they quickly discovered that the other mine was actually only a few feet away. Before they knew what was going on, they had broken through to another enormous cavern.

This might not seem like such a big problem, but over the years the abandoned mine had filled with water. When the miners broke through, all that water started rushing in to their mine. And there was no way to hold it back.

When the water started pouring through, the miners knew instantly what had happened. But there was no time to act. The lead miner radioed to another team and told them to run. But his team, the nine unlucky miners, had no time to escape. Before they could get their bearings, the escape routes had filled with water. There was no way out. And the water was rising.

They only had one chance: move to the highest point in the cavern and find an air pocket. They quickly did this, but they were still in terrible danger. The water was rising fast and it threatened to fill the whole cavern. They were already up to their necks. If it did that, the miners would certainly drown. But there was absolutely nothing they could do. They just had to hope someone above ground could mount a rescue before it was too late.

The rescue operation swung into action immediately after mining officials learned of the disaster. In a matter of minutes, the area above the mine was filled with doctors, mining engineers, heavy equipment, and countless volunteers who thought they might be able to help the rescue effort.

Obviously, the goal was to bring the miners out of the shaft as quickly as possible. But everyone knew that would take some time. Meanwhile, the mine officials had to do a few things to make sure the miners remained safe while the rescue was underway. First, the rescuers had to make sure that the nine miners had enough air. Second, they had to keep the miners warm—the water was freezing cold and the miners were at risk for hypothermia, a fatal condition that occurs when the body can't stay warm. Third, they had to reduce the water level. If it got higher, the miners were in danger of drowning.

The rescue team came up with an ingenious answer to these problems. It would take a lot of time to dig a hole big enough for the miners to fit through and escape. But it wouldn't be as hard to dig a smaller air hole. Rescuers immediately started drilling a tiny hole down to the trapped miners' air pocket. It took most of the night, but by the next morning—now Thursday—a tiny pipe had reached the miners and was pumping in air from above ground. The air pipe allowed the miners to breath. The air was heated, so the miners could warm up some. And the air was pressurized. This helped force down the water levels.

There was one other important thing

the airshaft did. The rescuers weren't in contact with the miners below as they were drilling. Rescuers were hoping for the best, but they didn't even know if the trapped miners were still alive. But the new air pipe helped answer that question. The miners below started tapping like crazy on the air pipe when it finally reached them. When the rescuers heard the tapping, they were overjoyed. Their friends were alive.

But despite their happiness, the rescue workers quickly settled down and got back to work. The next step was to drill an escape shaft. And they had to work fast. The air pipe was a temporary solution. Lots of things could still go wrong. The trapped miners had to be brought to the surface as quickly as possible.

Special equipment was needed to dig a shaft wide enough for the miners to escape. Rescuers had to have a drill 30 inches wide, and the closest drill of this type was in West Virginia. It would not arrive until Thursday afternoon. Until then, the rescuers had to sit tight.

Family and friends had gathered in the local volunteer fire station to wait. They watched activities on closed circuit television while they tried to comfort each other. The miners had children, wives, and parents hoping and praying for a safe return. Quecreek was a close-knit community and almost everyone in town knew one of the trapped miners.

But by this point, the story was no longer a local emergency. People all across the country were seeing it on television and hearing about it on the radio. It was a terrifying story and people were anxious for a happy outcome. It was a race against time. No one knew what was going to happen next.

Finally, at 2:30 on Thursday afternoon, the 30-inch drill arrived. Rescue workers started setting it up immediately. By 6 P.M. that evening, they were able to start digging. Experts estimated that it would take 18 hours to reach the trapped miners. If they drilled through the night, they thought they could reach the miners by the following afternoon.

At first, drilling went well. Volunteers and mining officials worked tirelessly to keep building the shaft. Contact had been lost with the miners—no one could hear tapping on the air pipe anymore. People just hoped for the best, and kept working. The rescuers were experts with this kind of thing. It was a difficult job, but if anyone in the world could get the trapped miners out, it was them. They just had to trust themselves.

The rescuers worked on past midnight, under the glare of the bright spotlights that lit up the rescue shaft. People were tired, but they kept going.

Suddenly, at 2 A.M., disaster struck. The end of the drill hit a hard rock and broke. Drilling quickly ground to a halt. No one could believe it. It had been a day of tragic luck, and things looked like they were getting worse. But no one stopped. They removed the drill, inspected the damage, and sent for new parts to get it fixed. It would be another delay, but no one was giving up.

✳

It took eighteen hours to get things underway again. An eternity for family and friends of the miners. And an eternity for the miners themselves.

The miners knew they were in trouble. But they also knew that they had a whole mining community behind them, struggling to get them out. The sound of the drill was proof of that. They could hear the 30-inch drill high above them, banging away at the rock. But when it stopped because of the breakdown, they couldn't figure out what was going on. For the next 18 hours they heard nothing but silence. It was a painful wait. They didn't know what was happening above.

Each one of the miners knew that he was facing death. They had a chance to escape. But it was just a chance. As they huddled together for warmth, they promised each other that they'd make it through. But in case they didn't, the men started writing final letters to their family members. Most were very simple. They told their wives and kids that they loved them. When the letters were done, one of the men sealed them in a lunch bucket. If the miners didn't make it, the waterproof bucket would, and their families would get their letters. It was a bleak thought. But they wanted to say goodbye.

Still, they never gave up hope. Even when things looked their worst. And when the drill started up again at 8 P.M. on Friday night, and they heard the loud machinery rattling and banging above them, they knew they were back in the game. They were cold, hungry, and frustrated. But the drill was working again. They had reason to be hopeful.

Back up top, the mood was equally hopeful. The delay had been agonizing. But now people were looking ahead. The drill was working. Time to get the miners out. But it was slow going. All through the night and into the next day, the rescuers worked a few feet at a time. They had to dig down nearly 250 feet. It was no easy task. But little by little, the drill moved closer to its target.

Again, they were not in contact with the miners at this point, so no one knew how they were doing. But rescuers were confident, and when they finally broke through at 10:20 on Saturday night, a phone system was immediately dropped down the shaft. The machines were still pumping and whirring, so it was hard to hear. But everyone's eyes were trained on the phone operator. For a while, he was completely motionless. He was straining to hear any sign of life from the miners. Suddenly, he cracked a huge grin and gave everyone a thumbs up sign. Then he put up nine fingers to let everyone know that all nine miners were alright. Cheers rose up across the rescue site. Back at the fire station, family members cried and hugged each other. The miners were alive.

A special elevator was inserted into the shaft, and one by one the miners were brought to the top. The first one appeared at the surface at 1:00 A.M., Sunday morning. Crowds gathered around and cheered as he emerged. The remaining miners followed, each time to wild applause.

The miners were cold, dirty, and exhausted when they reached the top. Each one was quickly placed on a stretcher and rushed to the hospital to be checked by doctors. Other than a few minor injuries, everyone was in great shape. The doctors were astonished.

But the medical exams were irrelevant compared to the reunions that were going on. Family members swarmed the hospitals to see the men they had almost lost. Children, wives, brothers, sisters all crowded into the hospital rooms to spend time with the miners. Everyone was laughing and crying, and grateful that the ordeal was over.

But the celebrations went further than just the hospital rooms. All around the United States, people were glued to their TVs, watching reports of the rescue. Just a few days earlier, newscasters told the bleak story of nine miners close to death 250 feet below the ground. Now they were telling the story of the happy and tearful families, reunited in the hospital. Everyone was calling it a miracle.

In the days that followed, the story was told and retold. Even President George W. Bush went to see the miners to hear their story firsthand. The president said the rescue was an example of the American spirit because everyone pitched in to help the miners, and because the miners never gave up hope.

The miners had other matters to attend to as well. Hollywood producers were all trying to buy their story. Everyone wanted to make the ordeal into a movie. But the miners were interested in simpler things. They were home. They were safe. And they were with their families. They smiled at the cameras and talked to the media and met with famous visitors. But mostly they wanted to eat dinner with their children, watch sports on TV with their friends, and do all the normal, everyday things they thought they'd never do again when they were trapped so far below the ground. The ordeal was over, and they were just happy to be alive.

I Escaped a Violent Gang

A Memoir as Told to Cate Bailey

Sometimes a true story can be more powerful than the most creatively written one. This true tale may be one. When Ana was 11 years old, she joined a hard-core gang in Long Beach, California. Below, in her own words, is the dramatic story of how she got out. She asked that we not use her real name or the name of her gang because she still fears for her safety and the safety of her family.

NOTE: Due to the mature content of this real story, you may wish to only share it with older listeners.

Gang members don't snitch on each other. That is the motto I was raised on. My dad once went to jail for something he didn't do because he wouldn't turn in a "brother." So when I was called to the witness stand that fateful summer day, I was planning to lie.

Paco, my main man from our Latino gang, was on trial. I'd seen him shoot and kill a teenage boy. John, a member of a rival, African-American gang, was also on trial. John was completely innocent. I was the only eyewitness, so what I said would determine which one went to jail.

The lawyer started asking me questions. I saw Paco sitting confidently at the defendant's table. He was calm because he was sure I would lie. I looked at John, and then John's mother. She was crying because it looked like her son was going to jail for a crime he didn't commit.

I started thinking about my mom and all the times she cried—when I got beat up, when my brother was arrested, when my dad got stabbed and shot at. I forgot about gang rivalries and prejudice. John's mother's tears became my mother's tears. I just wanted my mom to stop crying.

My eyes got watery and something happened inside of me. It went against everything I'd ever been taught my whole life. I told the truth. I said, "Paco did it!"

That was in 1994, when I finally got out of the gang. I couldn't go back after testifying against Paco. I was 15. But my story starts way before then.

I was raised in gangs. My father was in a gang; my brother was in a gang; my uncles and cousins were in gangs. I didn't know anything else. I thought drive-bys, drug deals, and beatings were normal.

When I was 5 years old, I saw one of my uncles shot and killed by a member of a rival gang. It took me a while to understand what had happened. I'd seen many people get shot before, but they were always taken to the hospital and then they came back. But my uncle didn't come back. At his funeral, I still didn't understand what was happening. I saw my mom crying, and she finally told me, "Your uncle's in heaven now."

After that, I got used to all the death around me. I attended many more funerals of loved ones lost to gang violence. And I watched my mom cry many more times.

I officially joined the gang when I was 11 years old. I got "jumped in," which means beat up by the other gang members. First, three girls surrounded me and hit me hard over and over. Then, all the girls in the gang made a circle around me and hit me and kicked me more.

Then, the guys came. About 20 guys lined up on one side and about 20 girls lined up on the other side, leaving a path down the middle. I had to walk through that path, as they punched and kicked me. And I had to be standing by the time I got to the end.

When I started down the path, my arm was already broken. It hurt so much. As I walked, they kept punching me in the ribs. Every time I fell down they'd kick me. I thought I was going to pass out. Toward the end of the path, I fell and they stepped on my leg and broke it. Somehow, I managed to pull myself up and limp to the end of the line.

That was my initiation. It was what I had to do to prove that I would do anything for them, even if that included dying.

A lot of people say that people join gangs because they want to fit in, but to me it was more of a survival tool. In my

neighborhood, you have to be from somewhere to be able to back yourself up. There were rival Asian and African-American gangs after our territory.

Before I turned 12, I'd been arrested for carjacking, violating curfew, and drug possession. Each time I was let go on probation. But when I was 13, I was arrested for possession of weapons. I got sent to boot camp for eight months.

Boot camp was the worst experience of my life. We had to get up at 5 A.M. and take cold showers and the rooms were always cold. The guards would stand right in front of me and scream stuff like, "You may be something on the street, but you're nothing in here."

For months, I had a bad attitude. I got into fights with other girls and talked back to the guards. They wouldn't let me see my mom until I improved my behavior. In the eight months I was there, she could only visit me four times.

When I got out on probation, I knew I never wanted to go back there. I had to attend school regularly, otherwise I'd be violating my probation and get sent back.

I hated school. I'd started "ditching" in the third grade. By junior high, I almost never went to school. I planned to drop out as soon as I got off probation. To me, my life was kickin' it with my friends.

My ninth grade English teacher, Ms. Gruwell, changed all that. She took an interest in me, asking where I'd been if I missed class and telling me I could be the first one in my family to finish high school.

I thought she was crazy. I thought she didn't know who she was talking to. I wasn't used to people being so nice to me. When you're in a gang, you think that nobody cares about you.

I told Ms. Gruwell to stay out of my business. But she kept at it. In my sophomore year, her words started to sink in. I began to see that there were other things out there besides gang life—that I could have a future, that I could graduate. I started thinking about getting out of the gang.

✳

For Ms. Gruwell's class, I had to read *Anne Frank: The Diary of a Young Girl*, the story of a teenage girl hiding from the Nazis during the Holocaust. Anne's words had a major impact on me. I came across the line: "I feel like a bird in a cage and I wish I had the wings to fly away." I couldn't believe it. *She* expressed exactly how *I* felt—I wanted to get out of gang, but they don't let people out. They kill people who want out.

That book really changed my perspective. Before I read *Anne Frank*, I was prejudiced against anybody I didn't know. I thought if you didn't look like me, you didn't understand me. But here was Anne, who was so different from me—she was Jewish and she lived 50 years before me—yet we felt the same.

I remained a "bird in a cage" until the day of the trial in 1994.

When I was called to the stand, I said, "Paco did it." I said it for myself, to get out of my cage. I said it for my mother, and for Ms. Gruwell. I said it to end the horrible cycle of violence in my life.

Paco looked at me in shock. As they took him away to serve his 25-year sentence, he said, "Of all the people in the gang, you're the last person I thought would betray me."

✳

I feel guilty to this day. I feel guilty that Paco is in a jail cell because of what I said, even though I know telling the truth was the right thing to do.

After I testified, I left the gang. I got death threats. But no one came after me. I think they didn't kill me for what I did and for leaving because I have family in the gang.

My mother doesn't cry for me or my dad anymore—my dad got out, too. My mom's very religious, and she thanks God for Ms. Gruwell everyday.

Today, I am freshman at a college in California. I plan to major in English and then get my Ph.D. in education. I want to be the Secretary of Education and change the way kids get labeled in school as a "dropout" or a "slow learner."

If gang members could see that they have different choices and that it's never too late to change, maybe they'd get out too. I'm not a miracle. Anybody can get out.

Frozen Alive

by Kim Feltes

How cold is really cold? What do you think the term "deathly cold" means? That's a question that a young boy has to answer in the story you are about to hear. And . . . as incredible as this story might be, remember it is absolutely true.

It was an icy December morning in 1987. Nine-year-old Justin Bunker climbed from his bed and glanced out at the snow-blanketed Connecticut countryside. He dressed, ate a quick breakfast, then made his way across the snow to a friend's house.

The two boys borrowed a sled from a neighbor. Then they headed to the playground of a nearby school. It had a great hill for sledding.

There was a shortcut into the playground. The chain link fence around an outdoor swimming pool had an opening in it. The boys climbed through. They were just making their way around the iced-over pool, but it was just too tempting. Justin and his friend skated out onto the thick ice in their boots. The two began horsing around. That's when it happened.

Without warning, the ice gave way under Justin's feet. He let out a yell as he shot down into the freezing cold water. His friend watched helplessly. He stared down into the dark hole through which Justin had fallen. Justin appeared to be on the bottom, face-up and not moving.

In a state of panic, the boy raced to Justin's mother, who called the fire department. Within six minutes, firefighters and paramedics arrived at the scene. Two of them immediately jumped into the frozen pool. Their heavy clothing and the darkness of the icy water made it hard to move rapidly. Several minutes passed before they reached the apparently lifeless body.

Finally, Justin was dragged from the pool. But there was no hope. He had been completely underwater for over twenty minutes. His eyes were frozen shut. His lungs and stomach were partly filled with ice-cold water. His body was stiff.

Justin was dead.

Well—he was almost dead.

Paramedics worked on him as they rushed him off in an ambulance. When he reached the hospital, he was unconscious and unable to breathe on his own. But he did have a faint pulse.

Doctors wrapped him in an electric heating pad. An oxygen mask was strapped over his face. For eight hours he lay in a hospital bed, unmoving, seemingly lifeless.

It seemed like Justin's life was slowly coming to an end. When suddenly he sat up in bed! Two nurses rushed to him. He pulled off the oxygen mask and tried to struggle free of the electric blanket. The nurses held his arms and tried to calm him. "Let go of me," he demanded. "What's going on? What happened?"

A few weeks later, Justin went home. He was healthy and normal in every way. That day, that frozen swimming pool, and his plunge to the bottom are just distant—and chilly—memories for Justin.

Do you find this story hard to believe? Do you find it hard to believe that someone could be completely underwater for more than twenty minutes and still live to talk about it?

It seems impossible, but it can happen. Here's why: When someone plunges into freezing water—just before that moment when freezing water is about to turn to a huge block of ice—he or she may be "quick-frozen." Blood vessels near the skin automatically shut down. The brain and other organs cool rapidly and need very little oxygen. The heart beats very slowly, and may even stop. Basically, the person is in a state of suspended animation.

That is what happened to Justin Bunker. And that is why he is alive and well today.

Autobiography in Five Short Chapters

by Portia Nelson

When one of the editors of this Read-Aloud Anthology first heard this poem that you are about to hear, it was being recited by an eighth-grade girl who had struggled throughout most of her years in school. But in seventh grade she began to work really hard. And because of her hard work, she made better grades. When she read this poem aloud, she introduced it by saying, "This poem reminds me of my life." As you listen to this poem, what do you think she meant by that?

CHAPTER 1

I walk down the street.
There is a deep hole in the sidewalk.
I fall in.
I am lost . . . I am helpless.
It isn't my fault.
It takes forever to find a way out.

CHAPTER 2

I walk down the same street.
There is a deep hole in the sidewalk.
I pretend I don't see it.
I fall in again.
I can't believe I am in this same place.
But, it isn't my fault.
It still takes a long time to get out.

CHAPTER 3

I walk down the same street.
There is a deep hole in the sidewalk.
I see it is there.
I still fall in . . . it's a habit . . . but,
My eyes are open.
I know where I am.
It is *my* fault.
I get out immediately.

CHAPTER 4

I walk down the same street.
There is a deep hole in the sidewalk.
I walk around it.

CHAPTER 5

I walk down another street.

Roger's Swim

by Don L. Wulffson

Sometimes you hear a weird and wacky story and you say to yourself, "I bet that could happen someday." And then there are other times you hear an amazing true story and you'll say to yourself, "Get out of here! That's not true!" Sometimes the strangest . . . and most amazing story is true. Such as the one you are about to hear.

It was a hot summer day in 1965. Four-year-old Roger Lausier was having a grand time. His parents had taken him to a beach near his home in Salem, Massachusetts. He collected shells. He made sand castles. And with his parent's attention turned away for just a moment, little Roger waded out into the water. Unfortunately, there was a sudden drop-off near the shore. Without warning, Roger was suddenly over his head. He tried to get back to the shore, but he didn't know how to swim. He tried to cry out, but instead he just swallowed water into his lungs.

The little boy knew he was drowning. But then something happened. A pair of strong arms was around him and he was being lifted out of the water. Luckily, a woman who had been swimming near the shore had seen Roger. That woman carried Roger to the shore.

On the shore there was much activity. Roger, who was now safe, was crying. Roger's mother was also crying. Both she and her husband blamed themselves for taking their eyes off their son—if only for an instant. They thanked the woman again and again.

Nine years later Roger returned to the same beach. He was now thirteen. He was big and strong for his age. And young Roger was also a good swimmer.

Spreading his towel on the sand, he suddenly heard a shout. It was cry for help. Beyond the breakers he could see a man fighting for his life.

Roger grabbed an air raft and quickly paddled out to the man. He reached him not a moment too soon. Roger helped the man onto the raft. Then, sliding into the water, he towed him safely to shore.

Later, Roger learned something very interesting about the man. His last name was Blaise. His wife was Alice—Alice Blaise, the very same woman who had saved Roger from drowning nine years before on the exact same beach.

Testing New Waters

by Sara Holbrook

Here is a poem that could be performed in a poetry slam. It compares a person's desire to take a risk—like trying out for a play or learning something new—with a stream of swirling water.

Safely standing
        on the bank of what-I-know,
unfamiliar water passing
        in a rush.
    If I jumped in,
        would I float?
    Or Sink,
        final as a flush?
  I could paddle like a dog
        and still wind up downstream.
What if I couldn't touch the bottom?
        What if no one heard me scream?

I'm shackled to this doubtful bank
        with maybes swirling in my ears.
  It's hard to judge the depth
        of an unknown stream of fears.

  Fresh water gurgles by,
        leaving me to wring my hands and look.
I could stand on what-I-know for life.
      or I
        could
          test
            one
              foot.

Homework Poems

Missing homework? Late homework? Teachers have it heard it all. In fact, it's a rare occurrence when a teacher hears a late or missing homework excuse that is truly new or unique. The following poems are a tribute to missing homework excuses. As you listen to them . . . does anything sound familiar to you?

Why My Homework Is Late
by Rebecca Kai Dotlich

Broke my nose.
Stubbed my toe.
Dropped my notebook in the snow.
Roof blew off.
Walls caved in.
Rusty scissors stabbed my chin.
Bit my tongue.
Choked on bones.
Caught a cold and kidney stones.
Had a boil.
Had a blister.
Had to babysit my sister.
Had the measles.
Had the pox.
Tonsils swelled up big as rocks.
Lost my watch.
Forgot the date.
And *that* is why my homework's late!

The Dog Ate My Homework
by Sara Holbrook

The dog ate my homework.
you've heard that before?
This one ate the table,
then chewed through the door,

Broke into the living room
with his munch mouth,
snacked on some carpet,
lunched on the couch.

He chewed up some albums,
then swallowed the mail,
even ate pretzels,
though they were stale.

He garbaged down everything
left in his path
and still wasn't full
when he found my math.

He chewed tops off bottles,
then drank all the pop,
as far as I know,
he still hasn't stopped.

If you don't believe me,
then give Mom a call,
if she still has kitchen,
or phone on the wall.

She'll answer and tell you
my story is true.
The dog ate my homework.
What could I do?

A Teacher's Lament
by Kalli Dakos

Don't tell me the cat ate your math sheet,
And your spelling words went down the drain,
And you couldn't decipher your homework,
Because it was soaked in the rain.

Don't tell me you slaved for hours
On the project that's due today,
And you would have had it finished
If your snake hadn't run away.

Don't tell me you lost your eraser,
And your worksheets and pencils, too,
And your papers are stuck together
With a great big glob of glue.

I'm tired of all your excuses;
They are really a terrible bore.
Besides, I forgot my own work,
At home in my study drawer.

The Plague

by Tod Olson

Late in the year 1347, Italians began to die from a terrible disease. It started with fevers, headaches, weakness, and loss of balance. Then came the ugly swellings in the armpits. Horrible pain struck on the third or fourth day. Arms and legs started twitching. And the fifth day, almost without fail, brought death.

By 1348, this plague had spread to France, Germany, and England. Towns and villages all across Europe fell apart. At its height, the plague killed 800 people a day in Paris alone. Parents left their dead children on doorsteps to be carted away. Dogs dug up bodies buried in mass graves. Crops were left rotting in the fields. Sheep and cattle wandered until they dropped from starvation.

We know now that the plague was carried by fleas that lived on rats. But at the time, no one understood the disease. The best medical minds weren't even close to inventing a cure.

No one in Europe had any idea what to do. So they looked for people to blame. In many places, that blame fell on the Jews. Thousands were forced from their homes. Thousands more were killed. But, of course, violence did nothing to slow the plague.

This is the story of an ordinary kid caught in the middle of this disaster. Christophe is a 15-year-old living in the south of France, in a town called Narbonne. He's an apprentice, or student. He's agreed to help a surgeon do his work. In exchange, the surgeon—his "master"—is teaching him to be a doctor.

Christophe is fictional. But the events that surround him actually happened.

There was a time when I didn't think I would live to tell this tale. Even now, ten years later, I remember the smell of death as though it were just outside my door. And when I want to push it away, I remember Master LaRoche's voice. He was my master, my teacher, my friend. And I hear him telling me to open my mind, even when it seems too painful.

I was 15 when I saw the first victim. It was in the summer of 1348, the brightest of days. I was in the field to the south of town collecting herbs for medicines. I heard the sound of hooves and looked up to see a rider draped like a blanket over his horse.

The horse walked slowly over the dirt toward town.

"You, there!" I called out. "Are you ill?" I was sure he was a trader who had come from the coast.

I got no answer and called out again. Still there was silence. I approached the horse and grabbed the reins. As I did, there was a terrible smell. The rider breathed in gasps. He was alive, and yet he stank of death.

Shaken, I left the day's work sitting in the field. I led the horse and her dreadful cargo quickly into Narbonne. It was market day, and the merchants and craftsmen were in the square selling their wares. People gathered around as I walked through. They were concerned about the man's health. But no one knew what it really was that I was bringing to town.

Jean Manon, the butcher's son, ran up to me and laughed. "Christophe! Your friend smells like our shop on a hot summer's day. You'd better salt him good before you sit down to dinner."

I managed a smile. "He'll be nothing but meat soon if Master LaRoche can't fix him."

"I saw your master this morning," he said. "I think he's helping someone on Tanner's Lane. That brown mare kicked a girl and broke her leg."

"Thanks," I said. I turned onto Tanner's Lane and found the right home. Master came out when he heard my cries. The rider groaned as we slid him onto the ground. His mouth fell open, and I could once again smell death on his breath.

Master LaRoche opened the man's shirt to give him air, and we gasped at the sight. Black spots covered his arms. His body appeared to be rotting like an apple. There were great swellings the size of

lemons in his armpits.

Master LaRoche stood up and turned to me. His face was grim. "It is here, Christophe," he said.

"It?" I asked. "What is here?"

"The plague," he said. "Last month, you may remember, a trader came to town from Messina with a horrible tale. He claimed people there were dying like pigs."

"But we thought he was crazy."

"Maybe he wasn't," he said. His eyes looked past me into the air. "Maybe he wasn't. . . . Help me drag this poor man inside, will you?"

A great cloud shut out the sun as we were dragging him off. By the time we reached the door, the skies had opened. A vicious rain poured down around us. I pulled my shirt over my head as though the drops themselves might contain poison.

The next day, we left him on a pile of straw in Master LaRoche's home. My master told his wife to spend the day outside, to be clear of the foul air. She refused, bless her soul. She stayed behind to pack herbs and mud on the patient's swellings.

We went out to make our rounds. That evening, we returned to a terrible sight. The trader's swellings had burst. The black spots had spread across his body. We buried the man that night. I never learned his name.

✳

Two weeks passed, maybe three, before I met Joseph. In those weeks, the plague had begun to spread its bony fingers around our town. At first, people refused to believe we were in danger.

Then, two Sundays after the trader's death, Charles the tailor stood up suddenly in the middle of church. He was sweating as he staggered toward the altar. His arms waved and twitched wildly. He made it to Father Marcus. Then he fell groaning on the floor.

I was too scared to move. I knew right then that whatever had killed the trader had escaped his body. It was in the air. Perhaps it was in the air in the church— the air I was breathing. I gasped and held my breath as long as I could.

Master LaRoche ran to the tailor's aid, along with the man's family. In a minute, I made myself follow. For a time, the rest of the church did not move. Then, someone got up and hurried out the door. The rest began to run as well. Many of them covered their mouths as they left.

The next day, I saw my friend Jean Manon. "Did you see?" Jean joked. "That tailor looked like a goose fleeing the axe."

He was laughing. And yet, I had noticed that he had nearly run over a child trying to get out of the church.

But I was writing about Joseph. . . .

At first, I did not want to go. But Master LaRoche made me come along. The streets were empty, even though it was midday. Charles had died shortly after that day in church. And since then, the master and I had seen more than 20 victims. People were keeping themselves shut inside, thinking they could keep the air pure.

I could feel eyes peering out of windows.

"Master, it is against the law," I said nervously.

"To treat the ill?" he said and looked at me with disapproval.

"Well, to bathe or eat or drink with Jews," I said.

"It is never against God's law—or any law I follow—to help people in need!" He began to walk faster.

"But what about the Christian children? Thomas, the merchant's son, told me they kidnapped a child in Avignon. Right under the Pope's nose! Then they nailed him to a cross, just like they did to Jesus!"

"Thomas told you that, eh? And did Thomas see it happen?" Master was angry now.

"No," I admitted. "He heard it from a trader. The trader had been in Avignon. He heard about it there. Everyone was talking about it."

"So, he heard about it from someone who heard about it from someone. And that person heard about it from someone else who probably heard about it too. We have a hearing problem in this land!" He was shouting now. A band of pigs eating garbage in the street looked up. They started and ran off.

"Why doesn't anyone believe in seeing?" Master continued. "Isn't it better to see what is true—not just talk about what might be? In all of France, I bet you cannot find a single person who has seen a Jew murder a Christian child!"

"But if so many people have heard about it . . . ?" I asked.

"That does not make it true!" my master responded.

"I still do not think we should be going there," I said stubbornly.

"Christophe, when your parents brought you to me, I had my doubts that you were ready to learn the art of medicine. Your head was young. But I had always thought your heart was good." His head dropped. "The first victim of this terrible plague is human kindness."

We turned into the Jewish Quarter. A mad flutter of wings frightened me. Three crows disappeared into the dark sky. On the ground lay three half-eaten rats, dead in the street.

Joseph's house was as big as any in town. It was two stories high, made all of stone. His father traveled often to Milan to trade for expensive cloth. He brought it back and sold it to anyone with the money to buy. "Christians may talk about the 'dirty' Jews," Master had said on the way over. "But they are perfectly willing to trade with them or borrow their money when it suits them."

Joseph's mother welcomed us at the door with a warm smile. Around her neck hung a six-pointed Star of David, made of silver. In a darkened room at the back, her husband lay moaning on a bed. Her younger son, Benjamin, lay on a mat nearby. Joseph, who appeared to be about my age, stood quietly in the corner, eyeing me. Everyone in the family wore a small yellow circle of cloth on their robes. The law says they must, so that no Jew can pass as a Christian.

Master and I sat by the bed. I pulled the poor man's shirt off. I had seen it a dozen times, and I still had to choke back a gasp. The swellings were already the size of apples. It was as though something evil—something very much alive—had taken over his body. For a moment I could almost feel it escaping through his open mouth and into mine. A cold shiver ran up my spine into my neck. Then I made myself concentrate.

We washed the swellings. Then we packed them with a dressing of clay. We did the same for Benjamin and started to pack our bag. Joseph's mother began to weep quietly.

Suddenly, Joseph spoke. "You're not going to bleed them?" he asked suspiciously.

"No," Master said. "It won't help."

"But you must do something to cool the body," Joseph insisted.

"Cutting them will make them weaker," Master said. "I bled Charles the tailor. A day later, he was dead."

"What can we do for them?" his mother pleaded. "Please tell me."

Master sighed and looked at his feet. "I don't know," he said sadly. "All our learning, all our books—nothing has prepared us for this."

"But, there must be something. . . ."

"I can only tell you what everyone knows. Eat onions, leeks, and garlic. Do not bathe; it opens the pores to let the poisonous air in. Keep southern windows closed; the disease is said to come from the south. Sleep on your side or stomach; it will keep the vapors from entering—"

"My older brother says bleeding cures," Joseph interrupted.

"Joseph . . ." said his mother, trying to quiet her son.

I could not keep silent anymore. "What does your brother know about medicine?" I asked. "My master is the finest surgeon in the south of France."

"My brother studies medicine at Montpellier," he said proudly.

"At Montpellier?" I tried to hide my surprise.

"Yes," he said, annoyed. "Even Jews can learn to practice medicine."

"I didn't mean—"

"My brother says we are the smartest students there," he said.

"I—I just didn't think they would be allowed," I stuttered.

"I guess there are some things Christians don't know," he said.

I was mad now. "We didn't have to come here! We could have . . ."

"Christophe!" Master called out.

"Enough! Let us leave these people alone." He picked up our bag, grabbed me tightly by the elbow, and yanked me toward the door.

He turned to Joseph's mother from the doorway. He lowered his voice so Joseph could not hear. "I feel I must tell you, Madame Simon. I have treated two dozen people so far. Not one was still living a week later. I'm sorry." And we went out into the rain.

✳

Thwack! Thwack! Thwack! The man next to me was beating his cane against the church pew. Philippe Martin was his name. He was a merchant. Light flickered off several bright silver bands around the stick.

Thwack! Thwack! Thwack! The crowd in the church began to quiet down. "I say lock them up!" yelled Martin in a voice like a crow's. "As soon as someone is stricken, lock him in his home!" The church started buzzing again, and he whacked his cane again.

My ear was beginning to hurt, when a great crash came from the altar. The church got very quiet. Father Marcus stood over the remains of a vase he had thrown on the floor. "Thank you," he said. "You cannot cure the plague by shouting it out of town."

He went on. "The town council has met. They have passed some laws to limit the spread of the disease. From this point forward, all bodies must be buried at least five feet underground. The town gate shall remain tightly shut.

"Only outsiders with essential business here will be allowed in. Any unmarried man and woman living together must marry.

"Above all, we must follow God's word.

And we must pray. Perhaps then He will have mercy on us."

Thwack! went the cane. "What about the Jews?" Martin cried out. I looked over. He was red as a tomato with anger.

Another voice from across the church called out. "They've poisoned the wells!"

I heard someone else yell, "Run them out of town!"

"Nonsense!" my master yelled, jumping out of his seat. "I have sat at the beds of at least ten Jews. They are dying as fast as everyone else. If they had poisoned the wells, would they be giving the water to their children?"

Suddenly, the red-faced man leaned over me. He lifted his cane and brought it down hard on my master's shoulder. He was muttering something I couldn't understand. Spit sprayed from his mouth onto my lap. He raised the cane again.

I stood up fast and caught his arm with both hands. Someone grabbed me and pulled me backwards over the pew. Thwack! I felt the sting of the cane on my arm.

I wrestled blindly. In a moment, I pushed my attacker onto the pew. I was shocked to find it was Jean Manon. He looked up at me with rage in his eyes.

Suddenly, a sharp tug at my arm sent me flying into the aisle. It was Master LaRoche. He pushed me toward the door.

We stepped out into the gray rain. I was hot with shame. My arm stung from the madman with the cane. We walked in silence for a minute. Then I said simply, "I am going home."

Master looked at me. "You are free to go at any time," he said. He sounded tired.

"You won't stop me, then?"

"You are nearly a man, Christophe," he said. "You will do what you feel you must."

"I can't take it anymore. Jean Manon was my friend—"

"When people cannot explain a tragedy, they must have someone to blame," he said.

We walked in silence. In a minute, we passed Jean Manon's street. His house was not far down, and I turned to look. At the door, I saw a strange-looking bundle.

"Come," my master said.

We walked up to Jean Manon's home. The smell from the butcher shop mingled with another all-too-familiar smell. I knew right away what I would find. I did not want to look. I did not want to breathe. If I ran fast enough, I thought, maybe I could outrun it. Maybe I could find someplace on earth that was free from this black death. Maybe I could stay alive.

Master pushed me gently forward. At the door lay a body, covered in a small blanket. I walked closer and made myself look. It was Jean's little sister, Marie. She just lay there, waiting for the gravedigger to carry her off. There would be no priest and no funeral. She might as well have been a rat.

The next morning, a knock came at the door. I opened it and found Joseph looking at me like a wounded deer.

"Is your master at home?" he asked.

"What do you want with him?" I stood blocking the doorway.

"I—I need to see him."

"You should not be here," I said. "You'll put us all in danger." He did not move.

"Christophe!" Master LaRoche came up behind me. "Who is it?"

I stepped aside. They looked in each other's eyes for a moment. Then Master said quietly, "Your father and your brother?"

"And my mother as well," Joseph said, wincing just slightly.

"You are alone now?" Master asked.

"Yes."

"Well, come in."

Joseph stood for a moment. He looked at me as though I were a guard dog.

"Come in," Master repeated. Joseph slid past me into the house.

They sat on wooden chairs in the front room. I stood in the corner, sullen. For some time, Master asked questions. Joseph nodded or shook his head in response. All the while, he hung his chin on his chest. He would not look up. Was his family properly buried? Yes. Did a rabbi attend them? Yes. Did he have more family in town? No. Did he have enough food? No. Money? No. Did he have a place to go? No.

All of a sudden, he lifted his head. He set his eyes on Master LaRoche. "I want to learn to cure people of this disease," he said.

Master looked at him with sad eyes. "I'm afraid I can't teach you that," he said. "I would do better as a priest. Then at least I could comfort them."

"My brother sent word the other day," Joseph said. "They are performing autopsies at Montpellier."

"The Pope is allowing it?" Master asked. "Perhaps you will learn something after all. But you should study there, not here. Go where reason is stronger than superstition."

"I am young," he said. "They won't let me in."

"Well, I suppose . . . Christophe here is planning to leave us," Master said. "I am going to need help."

"You cannot!" I protested. Master glared at me. Still, I went on. "Christians will not want a Jew to treat them."

"Then it will be their loss," he said.

"But you will put yourself in danger," I said. "You saw what happened at church."

"Everyone is in danger now," Master

said. "What does it matter if I add to it by doing some good?"

I looked at Joseph. Once again his head was bowed. He would not look at me. I pictured his mother weeping over his father's bed. And for a second, I saw my own mother's face in hers.

The air suddenly felt close and hot. I walked to the door. I pushed it open and ran out into the street.

I stood at Jean Manon's door for what seemed like an hour. His sister's body was gone. In its place lay a single, lifeless rat.

Finally, the door opened. I had not found the courage to knock. Jean stood in the doorway. "What do you want?" he said coldly.

"I—I saw what happened to your sister," I said.

He just glared at me.

"Your father and mother?" I asked.

"Nobody else," he answered. "Only Marie."

There was silence for a minute.

Finally, I blurted out a stream of words: "I wasn't defending them. It's LaRoche who is friends with the Jews. It was his idea to help them. I only went along to please him."

I heard the words come out of my mouth as though someone else were saying them. Shame began to rise through my body like bile. I wanted to run.

It had been two years since my parents had arranged for me to come here. Master LaRoche did not have to take me. He was known for miles around. He had his pick of apprentices. But he knew my father was ill. And he liked me. "Christophe," he said when my mother first brought me to town, "keep your eyes and your mind open, and we will get along perfectly."

Jean Manon spoke. "They did this,

Christophe. They killed Marie. A rabbi in the north has confessed. It was a plot from Spain. A boy carried the poison from Toledo, and the rabbi put it in the wells around Thonon."

"Did anyone see him do it?" I asked.

"No one had to see it. He admitted it," Jean said. "Twelve others helped him do it. And they are not the only ones. Martin told my father he saw Balavignus the Jew lurking near the southeast well the other day."

"Martin? That's the one who tried to hack off my arm with his cane."

"He is a very successful merchant."

"A successful brute, more like it."

"You should be careful who you speak ill of," Jean said. "And be careful who you keep as friends."

"What is that supposed to mean?"

"Things will get hard for the Jews on their Sabbath this week," he said. "And there has been talk about your LaRoche." Jean's eyes were set like an archer's staring down a bow at his prey. I began to get scared.

"What kind of talk?"

"That he is helping the Jews," he answered. "Some say LaRoche made the poison that they put in the wells. Others say he has been cutting open corpses, even though everyone knows it is unnatural. And the vapors escaping from the bodies have spread the disease further."

I felt my ears get hot with anger. "They have no gratitude! Where are all the other surgeons? They're gone. Or they hide in their houses. They are cowards, like most people in this town. Even the priests refuse to see the dying. And what about you? I saw you run from the church as fast as you could when the tailor took sick."

"So did everyone else," he said. The evil

look faded from his eyes.

"So did everyone else. . ." I repeated. I could not think of anything else to say. I simply turned and walked off. I left Jean Manon and the rat that lay where his sister once rested. And I walked.

I walked past the place where Charles the tailor once lived. I walked past Madame Bobeau's dogs, which no longer had an owner. I walked past a tiny wooden coffin the size of a small child. Finally, I came to the church and went in. It was dark and cool. I knelt in a pew and tried to pray, but my eyes would not stay open. I slept.

❋

I awoke to the sound of dogs snarling and barking. The pew was hard. My back was sore. Light was pouring through the eastern windows. I stumbled down the aisle and out into the morning haze. A dozen or so men were walking quickly down the street. Four angry dogs led them, straining at their leashes.

At the front of the pack, I saw a familiar gleam. It was the walking stick with the silver bands. Behind it marched Martin the merchant. He struck the cane hard on the ground as he walked. It was target practice, I suppose.

I did not know for sure where they were going, but I felt a pit in my stomach. I ducked down a side street to get around them. Then I raced toward my master's house. I reached the door in several minutes, gasping for breath.

I burst inside and bolted the door behind me. The front room was empty. I walked to the back room and pushed the curtain aside. The sight struck me like a dagger. Joseph sat on one side of the straw mattress. Madame LaRoche sat on the other. Between them lay Master LaRoche, sweat beading on his face.

I walked up to the bed and took his hand. He didn't move.

"He's finally resting," said Madame LaRoche softly. "It happened shortly after you left yesterday. It began the same way it did with the others. The staggering. Then the arms twitching. Then the fever. Now peace for a while."

"It can't be! Not him." Even with death all around us, I had somehow thought that Master LaRoche's kindness would protect him.

It was as though she could see my thoughts. "The disease doesn't care," she said. "It is blind."

I looked at Joseph. For a moment, I was angry. He was here while I was gone. He had helped my master to his bed. He had held the cool cloth to his head. What gave him that right?

I was about to speak when a sharp rapping came from the front door. Thwack! Thwack! And then the crow's voice: "LaRoche! Open the door, LaRoche!"

Madame LaRoche looked up, frightened. I stood up. "We can't let them in," I said. "They are here for Master LaRoche. Jean Manon told me. They think he helped the Jews poison the wells."

Joseph jumped out of his seat. He started for the door. I lunged at him and grabbed his arm. "What are you doing?"

"They won't come in here if they know he is sick," he said. "And they'll be content with me. They will have their Jew."

I let his arm drop and looked at him in shock. I could hear the dogs growling in front of the house. "But they'll put you in chains—or worse. . . ."

"What does it matter?" he said. He turned to say good-bye to Madame LaRoche. Then he disappeared into the front room and out the door. I ran to the window to see the dogs, teeth bared, snarling inches from his legs. The man with the cane stood in front of Joseph, sneering at him. Someone else tied his hands behind his back with rope.

They led him off, and I began to turn away. Then I heard a dull thud. I looked back to see the glint of silver in the air. Martin raised his cane a second time. Then he brought it down hard on Joseph's back. I winced and turned away again.

I sat that day beside Master's bed and watched the room darken. I wanted so badly for him to wake and tell me what I should do. I kept hearing his words: "The first victim of this plague is human kindness."

I pictured Joseph in jail. And I could not stop thinking that it should be me. What would they do to him? Accuse him of poisoning the wells? Burn him alive? They'd never stop to question why he was trying to learn to cure a disease he had supposedly helped create. Or why he would let his entire family die of it.

It didn't make sense. I couldn't understand why Jean Manon and the others did not see. And how could I not have seen?

Jean Manon had said that things would get hard for the Jews on Saturday. What did that mean? It was now Thursday.

I sat long into the night, watching Master's face. Finally, I felt my doubt slip away. The great knot in my stomach disappeared. I got up quietly and slipped out the door.

The jail was not far from the church where I had slept the night before. I walked fast, thinking furiously as I went.

I passed Jean Manon's street and turned in. His home was quiet. I slipped around to the back and paused at the door. It was the north side, and a window was open. I climbed inside and looked around. I picked up a large knife and a heavy iron crowbar and threw them out the window. They clattered as they hit, and a dog began to bark next door. I threw myself out the window, picked up my loot, and ran.

At the jail, the first thing I saw was the cane leaning against the front wall. Martin and another man—the jailer, I think—stood talking quietly. I hugged the side wall and crept around back. A window with iron bars was cut into the wall at shoulder height. Inside, Joseph crouched in a corner on the straw floor.

"Hey," I whispered.

"What are you—"

"Shhhhh. I'm getting you out." I wedged the crowbar between the bars and the wall. Then I braced my leg against the wall and pulled with all my might. The bars creaked loudly. I stopped and held my breath. I didn't hear a thing. I tried again, but the bars wouldn't move.

I heard Joseph's voice in a whisper. "There are keys inside on a shelf. If you can get the men away from the door . . ."

I thought for a minute, then crept around the side. From the corner, I heard pieces of conversation.

". . . bodies in wine barrels . . ."

". . . send them down the river . . ."

". . . tomorrow night . . ."

". . . quite a bonfire it will be . . ."

Then there was laughter.

Bonfire! I turned and ran to the church-yard. My heart was racing. I started to gather brush and twigs in the moonlight. Load by load, I crept back behind the jail.

In a matter of minutes, I had a pile as high as my head. I returned one more time and grabbed a torch. Even now, the priest was careful to keep one burning every night. I ran back and lit the pile. Smoke started to rise toward the sky. I ran to the other side and looked around the corner.

In a minute, Martin and the jailer began to sniff the air. They jumped up and ran around the building. As soon as they disappeared, I rushed inside. The keys were there. I unlocked the cell and Joseph ran out behind me.

We burst into the crisp fall air. Joseph ran. I looked down, grabbed the cane with the silver bands, and took off after him. We did not stop until we were standing in front of Joseph's door.

We sat at a large table in Joseph's house. Everything was exactly as it had been when Master LaRoche and I had been there.

We sat in silence for a moment. Then Joseph said, "How was he when you left him?"

"The same," I said with a sigh. "He didn't wake up."

"You know," Joseph said, "when he was crazy with the fever, he kept asking for his son."

"He doesn't have one," I said.

"He meant you."

I dropped my head and tried to swallow the lump rising in my throat. I looked at Joseph. He had torn the yellow circle from his shirt. Around his neck hung the Star of David that his mother had worn.

"You need to leave," I said suddenly. "I mean all of you. Everyone in the Jewish Quarter."

I told Joseph what I had heard at the jail. We spent the rest of the night going quietly from door to door. Not a person was surprised by our news. Husbands woke their wives. Mothers woke their children. And they all prepared to leave their lives behind.

Everyone seemed to know without thinking where they would go. They were off to Montpellier and Marseilles, to Spain and to Africa. They would live with cousins and brothers and uncles and friends. It was as if they had always known. And they had never let themselves feel at home.

The next day was quiet. Once again, the sun was blinding. All across the Jewish Quarter, people packed their belongings. In the shelter of their back courtyards, they loaded wagons. They loaded horses and mules. They took what they could carry. The rest they left behind.

After darkness fell, the procession began. Women and children rode. Men walked.

Joseph and I stayed behind long enough to see the flicker of torches bobbing up and down, headed for the Jewish Quarter. We stopped and sat on a hill a mile from town. The torchlight mushroomed into a larger glow as houses began to burn.

I turned to Joseph and touched him on the shoulder. We rose, turned our backs on Narbonne for the last time, and walked away.

Epilogue

As I write, I am sitting in the library of the university at Montpellier. I am 25 now. Joseph sits across the table from me. The plague is gone. So is about a quarter of the people of France. Other lands have suffered equally. The disease showed no favorites. Young and old, good and bad—they all died in massive numbers.

When Joseph and I left Narbonne, we went to my mother's village. Somehow, it had survived. They lost only their priest, a baker's daughter, and three old women. My mother took Joseph in without hesitation and showered us with love. For three years, we helped her tend her sheep. Then we went to Marseilles to make our own way. Thanks to Joseph's brother, we are here. And in two years, with our eyes and our minds open, we will both be doctors.

Understanding History: Why Were Jews Getting the Blame

This article explains how one group of people in Europe—the Jewish people—were unfairly blamed for the terrible events of the time. The writer of this article would like to ask of you—the listener—two questions: Why do events like this happen? How can we make sure that these kind of tragedies never happen again?

When the Black Death arrived in 1348, it devastated nearly every community. Fear and desperation were everywhere. People wanted someone to blame. They looked for villains outside the community. And in most parts of Europe, Jews were the outsiders.

For centuries, Jews had lived apart from Christians. They shared the same towns. But Jews lived in separate areas now known as ghettos. Laws often prevented Jews and Christians from marrying. In some places, Christians and Jews couldn't even drink wine together.

From time to time, Jews were allowed more freedom. They built temples and practiced their religion freely. Some Jews became skilled traders and became very successful. Most were educated.

But prejudice eventually won out. Some Christians resented the wealth of the Jews. Others believed horrible rumors that Jews kidnapped Christian children and murdered them.

Around the 11th century, Jews began to lose their freedoms. Usually, they couldn't own land or hold public office. Taxes were high, yet most jobs were off-limits. Some places forced Jews to convert to Christianity. Others kicked them out altogether.

When the plague hit, rumors started flying.

People said that Jews had started the disease by poisoning the wells. In one small German town, 11 Jews were tortured into confessing. They were put to death.

After that incident, towns in Germany and France began killing Jews or forcing them out of their homes. In one city, 200 Jews were herded into a wooden building and burned.

The Catholic Church did not officially support the killings. But the murders continued anyway. By 1350, Jews had been run out of nearly 200 towns. Thousands had been killed.

After the plague, it took 300 years for Jews to resettle in Germany. Then, in the 1930s, Germany—along with most of the world—sank into a terrible economic depression. Adolf Hitler and his Nazi Party came to power in Germany. And Jews were once again blamed for the country's problems.

From 1933 to 1945, Germans under Nazi rule herded Jews throughout Europe into prisons called concentration camps. There, about six million Jews were murdered.

The mass killings became known as the Holocaust. By far, this is considered one of the most evil and tragic events known to mankind.

Six centuries had passed since the plague. And no one seemed to have learned a thing. Why is that? And what can we do to make sure events like these never happen again?

The Birmingham Sunday School Bombing

The story you are about to hear is disturbing. It is about a bombing that took place in Birmingham, Alabama, in 1963. The bombing—and all of the racial hatred that surrounded it—shocked the nation. This is a magazine article that was written one week after the bombing took place. You'll notice that this article—because it was published in 1963—refers to African Americans as "Negroes," a commonly used term at that time.

Sunday morning, Sept. 15, was cool and overcast in Birmingham, Alabama. Sunday school classes were just ending at the 16th Street Baptist Church. Three 14-year-old girls, Carole Robertson, Cynthia Wesley, Addie Mae Collins, and 11-year-old Denise McNair were in the bathroom in the basement when the bomb exploded at 10:22.

Inside the church, a teacher screamed, "Lie on the floor! Lie on the floor!" Rafters collapsed. A skylight fell. Part of a stained glass window shattered. A man cried: "Everybody out! Everybody out!" A stream of sobbing Negroes stumbled past splintered wooden benches, past shredded song books and Bibles. A Negro woman staggered out of the Social Dry Cleaning store shrieking, "Let me at 'em! I'll kill 'em." Then she fainted.

White plaster dust fell gently for a block around.

Police cars poured into the block. Rescue workers found a seven-foot pile of bricks where the girls' bathroom once stood. On top was a child's choir robe. One worker lifted the robe. "Oh, my God," he cried. "Don't look!" Beneath lay the body of a Negro girl.

Bare-handed, the workers dug deeper into the rubble until four bodies had been uncovered. The head and shoulder of one child had been completely blown off. "Oh my God," screamed a girl. "That's my sister! My God—she's dead!" All four girls were dead. The law may have ended segregation. But hatred still lives on.

❈

The church's pastor, the Rev. John Cross, hurried up and down the sidewalk, urging the crowd to go home. Another Negro minister added his pleas. "Go home and pray for the men who did this evil deed," he said. "We must have love in our hearts for these men. Tomorrow we will have a rally for peace." But a Negro boy screamed, "We give love—and we get this!"

A man wept: "My grandbaby was one of those killed! Eleven years old! I helped pull the rocks off her! You know how I feel? I feel like blowing the whole town up!"

The Birmingham police department's six-wheeled riot tank thumped onto the scene. Cops began firing shotguns over the heads of the crowd while Negroes pelted them with rocks. Later, Negro youths began stoning passing white cars. The police ordered them to stop. One boy, Johnny Robinson, 16, ran, and a cop shot him dead. That made five dead and seventeen injured in the bomb blast.

Several miles away, two young Negro brothers, James and Virgil Ware, were riding a bicycle. Virgil, 13, was sitting on the handle bars. A motor scooter with two 16-year-old white boys aboard approached from the opposite direction. James Ware, 16, told what happened then: "This boy on the front of the motor scooter turns and says something to the boy behind him, and the other reaches in his pocket and he says Pow! Pow! with a gun twice. Virgil fell and I said, "Get up, Virgil," and he said, "I can't. I'm shot."

And so six died on a Sunday in Birmingham. The civil rights movement has a long way to go.

READER'S TIP

Ask students to share their feelings once they've heard this account. Ask them to imagine what it must have been like to live in Birmingham during this terrible time.

The Ballad of Birmingham

by Dudley Randall

The ballad you are about to hear was written soon after the horrible bombing of a church in Birmingham, Alabama, in 1963. Listen for the irony of how a child's tragic death was the result of her mother's wish to keep her safe.

"Mother dear, may I go downtown
Instead of out to play,
And march the streets of Birmingham
In a Freedom March today?"

"No, baby, no, you may not go,
For the dogs are fierce and wild,
And clubs and hoses, guns and jails
Aren't good for a little child."

"But, mother, I won't be alone.
Other children will go with me,
And march the streets of Birmingham
To make our country free."

"No, baby, no, you may not go,
For I fear those guns will fire.
But you may go to church instead
And sing in the children's choir."

She has combed and brushed her night-
dark hair,
And bathed rose petal sweet,
And drawn white gloves on her small
brown hands,
And white shoes on her feet.

The mother smiled to know that her child
Was in the sacred place,
But that smile was the last smile
To come upon her face.

For when she heard the explosion,
Her eyes grew wet and wild.
She raced through the streets of
Birmingham
Calling for her child.

She clawed through bits of glass and
brick,
Then lifted out a shoe.
"Oh, here's the shoe my baby wore,
But, baby, where are you?"

READER'S TIP

The effect of this ballad will be heightened if you pause between the first four stanzas, and before the last line.